Professional Management Consulting

At a time when consulting has increasingly come under scrutiny by governments and communities, *Professional Management Consulting: A Guide for New and Emerging Consultants* redefines "management consulting" and reinforces what it means to be a professional. With a focus on the importance of ethical practice and continuous personal development for building reputation, this easy-to-read book sets a new benchmark for aspiring consultants.

Based on sound research and supported by the author's background in leadership, management consulting practice, research, business strategy, and academia over several decades, Blackman brings together a range of tried and tested theoretical models commonly used by successful consultants. Drawing on his own experiences as a director of the industry's peak body, the International Council of Management Consulting Institutes, he provides a clear explanation on what a management consultant is and how and why clients use consultants to help them solve complex problems and manage change. With an emphasis on the importance of building and recognising relationships as a basis for problem-solving and implementing change, this book is an essential contribution to the profession worldwide.

This book is a vital resource for new and emerging professional consultants. It is suitable as an introductory text for business/commerce and engineering undergraduate students and a secondary reading for graduate students in engineering and management.

Alan J. Blackman is Director of the International Council of Management Consulting Institutes, a Churchill Fellow, and a CMC-Global Academic Fellow. He holds MBA and Master of Law degrees from Bond University and a PhD from Griffith University. This book is his third.

Routledge-Solaris Applied Research in Business Management and Board Governance

Series Editor: Charles Phua

Professional Management Consulting
A Guide for New and Emerging Consultants
Alan J. Blackman

Professional Management Consulting

A Guide for New and Emerging Consultants

Alan J. Blackman

LONDON AND NEW YORK

First published 2024
by Routledge
4 Park Square, Milton Park, Abingdon, Oxon, OX14 4RN

and by Routledge
605 Third Avenue, New York, NY 10158

Routledge is an imprint of the Taylor & Francis Group, an informa business

British Library Cataloguing-in-Publication Data
A catalogue record for this book is available from the British Library

Library of Congress Cataloging-in-Publication Data
Names: Blackman, Alan J., author.
Title: Professional management consulting : a guide for new and emerging consultants / Alan J. Blackman.
Description: Abingdon, Oxon ; New York, NY : Routledge, 2024. |
Series: Routledge-Solaris applied research in business management and board governance | Includes bibliographical references and index. |
Identifiers: LCCN 2024001205 (print) | LCCN 2024001206 (ebook) |
ISBN 9781032739649 (hardback) | ISBN 9781032739670 (paperback) |
ISBN 9781003466987 (ebook)
Subjects: LCSH: Business consultants. | Consultants. | Organization.
Classification: LCC HD69.C6 B54 2024 (print) | LCC HD69.C6 (ebook) |
DDC 658.4/6—dc23/eng/20240119
LC record available at https://lccn.loc.gov/2024001205
LC ebook record available at https://lccn.loc.gov/2024001206

ISBN: 9781032739649 (hbk)
ISBN: 9781032739670 (pbk)
ISBN: 9781003466987 (ebk)

DOI: 10.4324/9781003466987

Typeset in Times New Roman
by codeMantra

Contents

Figures

Tables

Acknowledgements

First, I would like to thank Steve Turner and Peter Westlund, Chris Cox, and the Institute of Management Consultants (Australia) directors for allowing me to indulge myself with this book. I also thank the ICMCI Board and executives for their insights, particularly Nick Warn (UK), Rob Bodenstein, Reema Nasser, and Dwight Mihalicz (Canada) for giving me a copy of his insightful book, "Consulting Through Uncertainty: A Global Perspective," from which I gained much. I also thank Dr Judy Lundy of Edith Cowan University and Peter Westlund for their review and editorial prowess and Michael McLean for his summary of International Standards. Finally, I thank my long-suffering partner, Karyn, for her support and love, without which I would be little. Thank you all!

Foreword

In 'Professional Management Consulting: A Practical Guide,' Alan takes the reader on a virtual journey to answer the question, "So, you want to be a management consultant?" Ticking off the key questions, Alan asks why a client organisation would want to use management consulting services, how to be a professional management consultant, and what the management consulting process is. Top of mind and close to my heart, Alan discusses the ethical practice of management consulting, a topic of some concern in recent years. He finishes with salient advice about the future of management consulting in a VUCA world.

Whilst this publication is almost mandatory for anyone contemplating a management consulting career, it also serves as a potent reminder for established and seasoned management consultants of the need for management consulting professionalism. Management consultants and the IMC need to promote the value of professionalism to satisfy society's expectations and deliver a high level of expertise. This publication reinforces this advocacy role on behalf of the profession [1].

Alan is articulate and concise in his delivery of the consulting essentials. The text is in an easy-to-read style that imparts clarity of thought to the discussed matters. Becoming a management consultant is not simply some years of experience in a specific discipline, topped with an MBA, and hanging up the shingle for clients to flock to the door. An essential requirement is a robust framework for offering management consultancy services, which is often overlooked. In Chapter 3, Alan dives into this requisite, leading with the IC-MCI Competency Framework developed for the certification of management consultants. In addition, there is a strong emphasis on being 'consultative,' a concept too often overlooked in the delivery of management consultancy services.

As a director of the International Council of Management Consulting Institutes, a Certified Management Consultant, and an Academic Fellow, Alan is uniquely positioned to articulate the requirements for being a management consultant. He points out that the publication is not a definitive description of management consulting models and analytical tools. However, this text contributes significantly to the why and how of management consulting practice. In doing so, it brings ethics to the centre of management consulting.

Peter Westlund
National President and Board
ChairIMC Australia
September 2022

About the Author

Alan Blackman is an Adjunct Associate Professor with Griffith Business School (GBS), a Director of the International Council of Management Consulting Institutes, a Churchill Fellow, and a CMC-Global Academic Fellow.

At the time of his initial retirement at the end of 2018, Alan directed the GBS Work Integrated Learning program. He taught Business Strategy as part of the school's MBA program from 1993 to 2011 and was Acting Director from September 2011 to April 2012. In 2012, Alan designed and implemented a range of local Business Internship and management consulting courses for GBS and, in 2014, created and convened a Global Mobility Business Internship program for the school. Also, that year, he received the Pro Vice-Chancellor (Business) Community Service Award for his outstanding contribution to the GBS community.

Alan earned Master of Business Administration and Master of Law degrees from Bond University in 1991 and a PhD from Griffith University in 2003. From 1992 to 2011, he managed Gold Coast management consulting and research company, the Centre for Independent Business Research, a business he founded. In 2010, he was recognised as Queensland's "Sports Volunteer of the Year" and in 2011 as Scenic Rim Region's "Citizen of the Year."

In 2014, Alan was appointed an Academic Fellow of the International Council of Management Consulting Institutes and an Emeritus Member for Life of the Australian Institute of Management Consultants. This book is his third.

Preface

> Some are born great, some achieve greatness, and some have greatness thrust upon them.
>
> (William Shakespeare, 1564–1616).

You've just finished your post-graduate program, wondering, now what? You think: "I know, I'll become a management consultant. I've all this new knowledge, and, on top of my ten years as a middle manager with a corporation and five before that working for the government, well, I'm a natural, aren't I?" Well, maybe.

So, what exactly is a 'management consultant'? Hmmm. What does one do? And, what personal qualities and other skills do I need? And how do I go about it? In most countries, you don't need a specific qualification to call yourself a "management consultant"0F0F[1], but you must be credible. So, what is management consulting, and what does it mean to be a professional?

The Institute of Management Consultants (Australia) requested this book. It, therefore, has an Antipodean slant but, hopefully, universal relevance. It aims to provide a clear and concise guide for consultants who are new to the field and seek to make the profession their career. It also aims to remind experienced operators of the fundamental principles and standards required of being a professional management consultant. Finally, it also is intended to be a source of insight for the purchasers of management consulting services.

Where relevant, the content aligns with ISO 20700:2017(E) and the International Council of Management Consulting Institutes' *Code of Professional Conduct* and *Competency Framework* (2021). It guides the reader towards ongoing professional development, international recognition, and ultimate certification. However, this book is not intended to be just an academic text. Nor is it a toolset for strategic planning, change management, or a book summarising the many international standards practitioners could and should apply[2]. They would be entirely different books. Instead, its purpose is to be an easy-to-read guide for those consultants who operate alone or are part of a small- or medium-sized consultancy and their clients, giving consultant and client insight into the profession and the processes and ethics of management consultancy. Enjoy!

Notes

1 Austria is an exception in which management consultants must be licensed through the Austrian Economic Chamber (WKO-Wirtschaftskammer). In other countries, management consultants operating in specific industries, such as engineering, may be regulated.
2 A list of just some of the international standards is included as Appendix F to this book. My thanks to Michael McLean of IMC Australia for the content of that list.

1   The Profession

> The farther back you can look, the farther forward you are likely to see.
> (Winston Churchill, 1874–1965)

The Beginnings

Management consulting emerged as a viable industry in the late 1800s during the second phase of the Industrial Revolution. Perhaps best known of the consulting pioneers was an American engineer and the father of the Scientific Management movement, Frederick Winslow Taylor (Figure 2).[1]

Notable exponents of the scientific approach were engineer and consultant Frank Gilbert and psychologist and industrial engineer Lillian Gilbreth, whose work on efficiency, time, and motion became the foundation for mass production.

Dr Arthur Little of the Massachusetts Institute of Technology (MIT) opened the first management consulting firm in the 1890s. McKinsey &

Figure 2 Frederick Winslow Taylor (1856–1915). British Library collection.

DOI: 10.4324/9781003466987-1

Company of Chicago is the first and longest-running strategic management consulting firm in the United States. Under the direction of James McKinsey and Marvin Bower, "McKinsey & Company led the way for the management consulting industry by incorporating professional standards, much like those of the legal and medical professions" [2, p. 4].

Following World War II (1939–1945), an economic boom and increased competition encouraged more analytic and strategic management consulting firms. As a result, early management tools started to appear; the most notable was a process developed by Harvard University in the 1950s for analysing business strengths, weaknesses, opportunities, and threats, now known simply as the SWOT analysis. In addition, other tools were transferred from earlier military use to management. A significant one was analysing an organisation's political, economic, social, and technological (PEST) environment. Over time, this was extended to include environmental and legal aspects.

Over the next three decades, management consulting organisations and business schools – such as the Boston Consulting Group, McKinsey & Company, and Harvard Business School – set the stage for today's consulting industry by developing analytic tools for strategic decision-making. At the same time, large accounting firms (e.g. the former Arthur Andersen) and information technology firms (e.g. IBM) developed their consulting divisions, giving rise to the diverse and formidable management consulting industry we experience today.

In Australia, management consulting began during the post-World War II economic boom based on the experience of American and British consultancy firms. The first Australian management consultancy, W.D. Scott & Co, was established in Sydney in 1938. It used industrial engineering techniques to improve labour costs and shop floor productivity. Building on US consulting expertise, it established a significant consulting business, later contributing to the global diffusion of efficiency methods. By the 1960s, it had become one of the largest management consulting firms in the country. Another early innovator was the British consultancy Personnel Administration, which established an Australian branch in 1948, also providing industrial engineering services. Manufacturing growth during the 1950s and 1960s led to expanding consulting services focused on productivity improvement and personnel management.

In the 1970s and 1980s, new segments of the consulting industry emerged in Australia. The entry of major accounting firms, such as Price Waterhouse, Coopers, Lybrand, and Arthur Andersen, into management consulting services was valuable. For example, Arthur Andersen, focusing mainly on computer and information technology consulting, emerged as one of the major players in the Australian consulting industry, later spinning off its consulting division as Andersen Consulting (now Accenture).

McKinsey & Co. established an Australian presence in Melbourne in 1962 and a Sydney office in 1971, mainly working for local subsidiaries of global clients. During the 1980s, McKinsey's Australian offices flourished, and the firm became the consultant for the chief executives of the country's largest companies. In addition, the growth of the financial services and resource sectors during the 1990s resulted in other U.S. strategy firms establishing Australian offices, including Boston Consulting Group, Bain, and Booz Allen & Hamilton.

The Australian management consulting industry underwent a significant structural change through new entrants and existing companies' mergers. By the 1990s, the contemporary structure of the industry had been established around a small core of sizeable global consulting firms and a growing periphery of small specialist providers. While most of the large consulting companies emphasised their expertise in areas of business strategy, the primary growth in consulting activity occurred in more operational areas such as information technology, cost reduction, business process re-engineering, and human resource management. Barry [3] identified the industry drivers of management consulting in Australia as the total number of businesses in the market, total business profit, private and public sector capital expenditure, demand from finance, and business confidence. However, Haslam and his team found that the most robust predictor variables for the size of the management consulting market in a country were its gross domestic product, gross domestic product per capita, Hofstede's Individualism score, the eGovernment Index, and the V-Dem Electoral Freedom Index [4–7].

The Institutes

Institutes of Management Consultants

As a professional management consultant, you become part of a global community of "trusted, ethical, and committed individuals" [8]. The first professional institute for management consultants was established in 1940 in the Netherlands [8]. There are now institutes of management consultants, or IMCs, found in 48 countries (Appendix A). In addition, a global institute has been created to cater to the needs of those consultants based in countries for which no IMC has yet formed.

The primary role of an IMC is to certify and recertify qualified members, that is, individual consultants, according to internationally agreed standards of professional behaviour and competence. Other functions include promoting the profession, setting and maintaining professional standards, providing members with professional development and networking opportunities, handling complaints, and resolving disputes. Members who achieve certification are recognised worldwide as "Certified Management Consultants" and entitled to use the postnominal "CMC." However, before certifying its members, an IMC must be accredited by a volunteer-driven international body, CMC-Global. More on that later.

The Australian Experience [9]

In 1966, "The Australian Management Consultants Association" was established. It consisted of accounting organisations and two or three larger consultancies and focussed on large practices with no apparent interest in smaller consultancies or sole operators. However, foundation members of the then-current institute saw the necessity to form a separate group, offering membership to consultants from large and small organisations and sole operators who met the appropriate qualifications and agreed to a standard of ethics. Accordingly, following regular monthly meetings of interested consultants in the Sydney suburb of Crows Nest in 1966 and 1967, an application was lodged to register the "Australian Management Consultants Group (NSW Chapter)."

President John Searcy-Hammond was credited with doing most of the hard work drafting the Memorandum, Articles of Association, and Code of Ethics, which were redrafted by solicitors and submitted for registration [9]. Finally, on 18 September 1969, the association was incorporated as a company limited by guarantee [10]. The first general meeting was held on 5 January 1970, with 37 financial members. Colonel Urwick, a British Management Consultants Association co-founder, was the guest speaker – his topic: "The Consultant as a Matchmaker" [9].

In February 1970, an invitation was sent to P.A. Consulting, P.E. Consulting Group Australia, and W.D. Scott to meet with the Council of the institute. The Council's view was that institute membership by consultants from the three leading companies could benefit consulting and consultants in Australia. The meeting did not occur then, but by 1972, several consultants from the three organisations had become members. Also, in 1972, consultants in other states, particularly Victoria and Queensland, expressed their interest in joining as members of the New South Wales (NSW) Association. That interest assisted the development of organisations in both of those states. As a result, the association's name was changed to "The Institute of Management Consultants in Australia Inc" on 22 December 1972.

That year, Price Waterhouse's managing director undertook for his company to pay membership fees for 30 consultants for three years. In addition, the institute's chairman announced that the organisation would encourage its member companies' consultants to join the institute. As a result, Alf Paton of P.A. Consulting became a member and advised that his firm's consultants would be encouraged to join. Another letter was forwarded to B.W. Scott of W.D. Scott & Co, inviting him to join. Following the institute's representations and recognition of the industry's growth, the dominant business directory of the time, Pink Pages, ceased listing Management Consultants under Employment Agencies and instead listed them under a new discreet heading. By 1974, the institute had grown to 164 members. The first professional development conference was held in September of that year.

By 1976, the College of Principals within the IMC was formed. State chapters were created in Victoria and Queensland, and consultants in Adelaide and Perth expressed interest in developing branches in their states. Using the established entity, throughout the late 1970s and early 1980s, the movement grew into a federation model that included state chapters.

Since then, the Australian IMC has grown considerably and operates chapters in Australia's six states and two territories. It is a membership-based not-for-profit company limited by a guarantee [11]. A national board of directors manages it and collects fees from its members. The board has three committees to consider and advise on strategic, operations, and governance issues: Finance, Risk, Audit, and Governance; Membership; and Professional Development.

Since 2020, IMC's object has been to:

Promote excellence and integrity in the management consulting profession, to improve the knowledge and skill of management consultants with respect to their roles, duties and responsibilities and to encourage and require the highest professional standards and ethics among management consultants.

[11, p. 4]

In October 2003, the IMC Board affirmed that the institute exists to further the interests of management consultants and clarified the definition of management consultants as: "Objective professionals who provide advice and assistance in the process of management across national boundaries." It determined that the IMC should support management consultants by:

- providing advocacy,
- maintaining professional standards,
- promoting the image of the IMC and the CMC brand,
- supplying attractive fee-for-service member services, and
- identifying business development opportunities.

As well as being a member of the International Council of Management Consulting Institutes (ICMCI), the institute is a Professional Association member of the Australian Council of Professions, the peak body representing professions in Australia. In that role, the institute must "assist in promoting the professions and professional advice, maintain professional standards and ethics, and develop the profession" [12].

The Market Size of Consulting in Australia

Australian consulting has come a long way since the 1960s. From 2007 to 2012, the local industry experienced growth rates of 2.1% per annum, generated annual profits of AU$927M and paid wages of AUD4.2B. However, the industry's size is hard to pin down, partly due to differences in research methodology and industry definition. For example, by March 2023, IBISWorld estimated that the sector had grown to 90 thousand management consulting businesses and employed 158 thousand people. Industry revenue had increased to AU$43.4B and generated a profit of AU$5.1B [3]. However, in contrast, Source Global Research found the size of the Australian management consulting market in 2022 to be "around US$7.2 billion" [7, 13], while ICMCI's own National Consulting Index estimate for that year was for a market size of US$9.1 billion. Further, an analysis of "Management and Related Consulting Services" entities registered on the Australian Business Register in June 2022 identified 29,189 businesses. Given the differences in findings, there is a clear need for researchers to agree to and adopt a standard definition of what a professional management consultant is and is not to fully enable professional bodies and governments to understand the industry's economic importance.

International Council of Management Consulting Institutes (ICMCI)

Over time, consultants in individual regions came together to form local IMCs. The Australian IMC played a vital role internationally by fostering such cooperation. From 10 to 12 May 1987, 32 management consultants from ten countries met in Paris, France, to explore the common ground between those institutes known to certify individual management consultants. As a result, seven of the ten agreed to form an international body to work towards establishing reciprocated standards for the evolving profession. The Australian IMC was one of seven founding professional institutes of the ICMCI. Other founding institutes were from Austria, Canada, Denmark, South Africa, the United Kingdom, and the United States. After two days of meetings, the delegates proposed the ICMCI's formation as an apolitical, not-for-profit peak industry body to improve and standardise the worldwide certification of management consultants [14]. The organisation's first Chair was the United States' John D. Roethle, and the vice chair was the United Kingdom's Thomas Hedley [14]; Canada's David Amar was later appointed as a second Vice Chair [15].

At the Paris meeting, study groups were formed to achieve five specific short and medium-term objectives for the new organisation. Tasks set for the groups included identifying and analysing other institutes of management consulting and certification bodies, developing standard international definitions for "management consulting" and "management consultant" and for "Full or Regular/Certified Membership", compiling an inventory of common national bodies of knowledge, developing a process for sharing information and liaison between institutes, and drafting an international code of professional conduct. In addition, it was agreed to appoint an officer or board member from each institute as its official liaison to the Council [14, p. 2].

A second meeting was arranged and held in Dusseldorf, Germany, in 1988, at which it was decided to have an international congress every two years. By the May 1989 Congress in Copenhagen, Denmark, ICMCI's organisational structure was in place, including membership requirements and application processes. Membership had grown to 11 IMCs following accepting applications from Italy, the Netherlands, New Zealand, and Sweden [16]. The 30 delegates from the 11 countries who attended this session ratified the structure and membership criteria, agreed to establish ICMCI as a Swiss verein3F3F,[2] and approved the ICMCI Code of Professional Conduct. This ICMCI Code thus became the first international code of conduct for any profession. The Copenhagen Congress also established the basis for reciprocity of CMCs between ICMCI member institutes [17]. It elected a new Board for a three-year term chaired by Thomas Hedley, with Vice Chairs David Amar and the United States' Michael Shays. Australia's Geoffrey Smith was appointed Secretary, and Europe's Otto Leissenger, Treasurer. John Roethle remained the Past Chair to facilitate a smooth transition [15], a practice that remains today.

In 1993, the ICMCI members agreed to execute its strategic plan, which focussed on the following six goals:

1 Developing international standards that are supported and adopted by member institutes.
2 Gaining global recognition of the organisation as the industry's peak body and the CMC designation as the benchmark "of management consultancy competence, objectivity, independence, and professionalism" [8].
3 Increasing membership by encouraging all appropriately qualified certifying institutes worldwide to join ICMCI.
4 Supporting current and potential members by providing appropriate networking, knowledge sharing, and promotional activities to increase the memberships and recognition of individual Member IMCs.
5 Raising sufficient funds from Member IMCs to cover ICMCI's running costs and identifying and developing other funding sources to achieve the organisation's mission and vision.
6 Enhancing organisational effectiveness through cost-efficient methods and structure.

ICMCI held annual meetings from its outset [18], and the body continued to grow. New boards were elected every three years. A critical moment in ICMCI's history was the appointment of a full-time Executive Officer, Reema Nasser, in 2013 and the establishment of a forum for academics to share ideas and research around professional management consulting. Following, on 15 June in the same year, the organisation held its first international conference for CMCs in Lithuania – Vilnius (Figure 3). Except for 2020, when the COVID-19 pandemic prevented travel and face-to-face gatherings, international CMC conferences have been held annually since 2013, coinciding with the yearly delegates' meetings.

In 2001, the ICMCI held its eighth Congress in Sydney. Conference materials included the adoption of assessment standards for awarding CMC

Figure 3 From L to R, Robert Bodenstein CMC, Toni Brunello CMC, and Reema Nasser(Executive Director) at ICMCI's first CMC International Conference. Photographer Ligita Vaitkute, 2013. Published with permission.

certification. An ICMCI "Code of Professional Conduct" was also proposed at that meeting. However, some major accounting and consulting firms considered their standards superior to the international body's and withdrew. Despite that setback, congress participants adopted the ICMCI's code, making ICMCI the first international peak industry body for advisory services to codify professional conduct worldwide. At the time of writing, the more prominent accounting and consulting firms remain outside the ICMCI network [19].

In 2004, ICMCI undertook an international assessment process to ensure that CMC certification is based on a common standard visibly and credibly validated against the Code in each member country. As a result, ICMCI has established a firm basis for professionals holding the CMC designation to gain worldwide reciprocity. Since that assessment, ICMCI's Quality Assurance Committee has assessed each Member IMC every three years to ensure that each institute's CMC standard is equivalent to the professionalism and ethics required of CMC candidates [20]. In addition, driven by the ICMCI, in 2017, the International Standards Office (ISO) published ISO 20700:2017 to provide a set of universal guidelines for delivering management consulting services.

In 2012, ICMCI was rebranded as "CMC-Global" in recognition of the increasing number of Certified Management Consultants (CMCs) in its network [8]. As shown in Figure 4, CMC-Global (ICMCI) has a simple bottom-up structure driven by its IMC members, all of which are not-for-profit bodies whose membership consists of individual consultants and consultancies. Delegates from each full member IMC elect a board of nine to set the organisation's strategic direction and control its operations. Elected for three years, the directors are unpaid volunteers who report to an Assembly of Delegates as a board. The board of nine meets at least monthly, and the Assembly of Delegates annually. Only CMCs representing paid-up Members of CMC-Global are eligible to stand for the board.

As Figure 5 shows, CMC-Global's network is worldwide. With 46 national IMC Members, the organisation now represents consultants from 82 countries. In addition, the Academic Fellows Faculty now numbers more than a hundred primarily professorial-level academics from universities around the globe. Regular yearly meetings bring institutes, academics, and their members together to share experiences and research (Figure 6), thus ensuring that members are updated with current trends and issues affecting the industry and their clients. A complete list of IMC Members and their email addresses can be seen in Appendix A.

CMC-Global's network includes several international bodies. For example, in July 2001, it was granted Special Consultative Status by the United Nations Economic and Social Council (ECOSOC). Links have also been forged with the European Bank for Reconstruction and Development (EBRD), the International Organization for Standardization (ISO), the European Committee for Standardization (CEN), the Italian Organization for Standardization (UNI), the International Accreditation Forum (IAF), and the United Nations Industrial Development Organization (UNIDO).

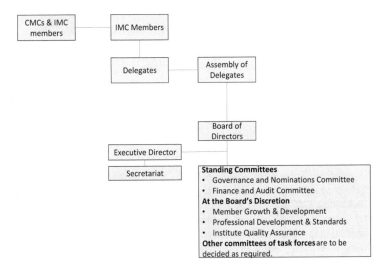

Figure 4 CMC-Global's organisation structure in 2023.

Figure 5 CMC-Global's network of national IMCs.

Figure 6 CMC-Global annual meetings and events from 1987 to 2023 (2021 and 2022 were virtual meetings).

As shown in Figure 7, ICMCI/CMC-Global has been widely supported by its members. Since its formation in 1987, 25 IMCs, spanning five continents, have been represented on the Board. Appendix B lists the Board members by nominating IMC and their various positions.

Since 2013, CMC-Global has transitioned from a volunteer-operated organisation to a volunteer-directed one [21]. The 2023 Board comprised representatives from nine countries and four continents (Figure 8).

However, despite broad membership support, financial constraints have meant that smaller IMC members, or those geographically distant from

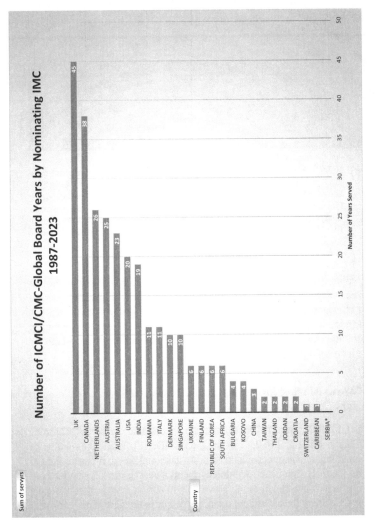

Figure 7 The number of years of Board representation by the country of nominating IMC.

Figure 8 ICMCI Board in March 2023. L to R: Dwight Mihalicz (Canada; Immediate Past Chair), Norma Shorey (The Caribbean), Alan Blackman (Australia), Gergana Mantarkova (Bulgaria), Jehona Lluka (Kosovo), Tamara Abdel-Jaber (Jordan; Treasurer), Nick Warn (UK; Secretary), Ruggero Huesler (Switzerland), Robert Bodenstein (Austria; Chair), Reema Nasser (Jordan; Executive Director), Khuzaima Zaghlawan (Jordan, Executive Secretary). Amman Jordan, 22/03/2023. ICMCI with permission.

CMC-Global's administrative centre, have hesitated to nominate one of their own to stand for a position on the board. That constraint limits the organisation's management diversity. However, as CMC-Global continues to grow and develop its network, financial limitations are expected to ease, opening up opportunities for the smaller and distant members to participate more actively in the industry's governance.

The World Market for Professional Management Advisory Services

Source Global Research (SGR) estimated the world market size in 2022 to be US$228,805 million, or 0.23% of the global GDP [7]. While the number of individual management consultants worldwide is unknown, it is sufficient to assume that it is significant. As already mentioned, the market size for consulting services is difficult to pin down due, in part, to a lack of consistency in how data are collected and reported, as well as in the definitions of what a management consultant is and is not.

To define the consulting market size in each country, ICMCI started a research project in 2018 to determine the factors influencing the national market size and to develop a mathematical model for calculating each country's contribution to the global supply of management advisory services. Known as the National Consulting Index (NCI), the NCI formula, which is still under development at the time of writing, has been based on a linear regression of correlated factors against benchmark country data purchased from SGR.

While the research is ongoing, what is clear is that a key influencer on the size of the Management Consulting Sector (MCS) in each country is the size of the national Gross Domestic Product (GDP). A country's GDP can explain a quarter of variability (*Part R^2* 0.27) in the regression model. However, it's not that simple. Other effects come from, for example, the level of innovation and the uptake of technology in a country, the degree of economic freedom available for trading, cultural differences, and the average education level of the national population. Other factors are being investigated and may yet be shown to have notable effects. Of course, market sizes vary considerably across national borders. However, from the data available for CMC-Global members for 2022, the median MCS was US$680 million that year.

In all, 82 counties come under the ICMCI banner. So far, three calculation methods have been used to estimate national MCS size: data purchased from SGR, the NCI formula, and assessing the market size as a percentage of GDP. For 14 countries, no estimate has been possible so far due to a lack of GDP or other data. For the remaining 68, data were bought for 14 countries, MCS sizes for 25 were estimated using the evolving NCI formula, and GDP was used as the basis for the remaining 29. At the time of writing, all estimates are being reviewed and compared to those of individual IMCs. However, SGR's MCS size estimates for 2022, adjusted by 25% [22] to include the contribution of small and medium-sized consultancies for the 14 countries for which data were purchased, are listed in Table 1.

Table 1 Source Global Research estimates of Management Consulting Sector (MCS) size as a proportion of national GDP in 2022, adjusted by plus 25% to include the contribution of small- and medium-sized consultancies

Country	GDP2022 (US$M)	MCS (2022) (US%M)	Estimate type	Percentage of national GDP
United States	25,035,164	137,511	SGR+25%	0.55
United Kingdom	3,198,470	27,353	SGR+25%	0.86
Germany	4,031,149	22,680	SGR+25%	0.56
China	18,321,197	18,309	SGR+25%	0.10
Australia	1,724,787	8,969	SGR+25%	0.52
Canada	2,200,352	7,774	SGR+25%	0.35
Japan	4,300,621	7,033	SGR+25%	0.16
Netherlands	990,583	4,183	SGR+25%	0.42
Italy	1,996,934	4,045	SGR+25%	0.20
Brazil	1,894,708	3,741	SGR+25%	0.20
Singapore	423,632	2,971	SGR+25%	0.70
Türkiye	853,487	1,605	SGR+25%	0.19
Austria	468,046	1,551	SGR+25%	0.33
South Korea (ROK)	1,734,207	1,011	SGR+25%	0.06
			Mean	0.37
			SD	0.24

Now that you have some background on the profession and the organisations supporting it let's explore the roles of a professional management consultant and why a client organisation might seek to engage a person or firm to advise it.

Notes

1 For more on Taylor and his relevance, see https://hbr.org/1988/11/the-same-old-principles-in-the-new-manufacturing.
2 A Swiss verein is a type of business structure that allows different business types to merge. The English translation is simply, **association**. For more on this, see: https://swissfirma.com/open-swiss-verein/#:~:text=A%20Swiss%20verein.

2 The Roles

> Being a professional is doing the things you love to do, on the days you don't feel like doing them.
>
> (Budd Mishkin) [23]

What Is Management Consulting?

Management consulting is an independent advisory service contracted to improve organisational performance, address management challenges, help solve management problems, identify and assist clients in taking full advantage of growth opportunities, and assist with implementing change. It is a dynamic and rapidly evolving profession requiring individual consultants to reinvent themselves constantly to maintain relevancy.

Smith [24] suggested that "consulting is aimed at some improvement in the future functioning of the client system—that is, positive change" and that the purposes ... are to provide "... a specialised expertise, content, behaviour, skill or other resources to assist/help a client in improving the status quo. This intervention focuses on a specific client need."

Organisations are seeking consultants who are experts to help problem solve. Smith [25] described an expert as "competent, qualified, and principled." Relevant across all sectors, competency is at the core of professionalism and will be discussed in more detail in the following chapter. However, qualification tends to be specific and is not limited to an academic standard. It includes particular industry knowledge and skills garnered over time, skills that are current. Maintaining knowledge and skills currency will be discussed in more detail in Chapter 9.

Being principled involves sticking to one's beliefs, having a moral framework encompassing integrity, honesty, and trustworthiness, and applying ethical principles in decision-making. Ethical practice is also at the heart of professionalism; the principles will be covered in Chapter 8, while the Code of Conduct and Consultant's Pledge are in the appendices of this book.

DOI: 10.4324/9781003466987-2

In all, there are 12 traits essential to being a professional consultant [24, 26, 27]:

1   Integrity and honesty – the commitment to act and advise within an ethical framework.
2   Balanced – a stable personality with well-developed interpersonal qualities and skills.
3   Independence – always committed to providing objective advice.
4   Curiosity – always looking to fill in the gaps in their knowledge.
5   A clear communicator – as a questioner, listener, speaker, and a writer.
6   Trained and experienced – resulting in expertise in specific management functions and issues, plus an overall breadth of knowledge across functional management areas.
7   Intuition and awareness of the current challenges being faced by organisations and their management, as well as of emerging trends and technologies.
8   Proficiency in problem identification and critical thinking – with the ability to use appropriate diagnostic and analysis tools and techniques.
9   Skilled at "dilemma solving" [27] and at working with ambiguity – of finding innovative solutions to "wicked problems" [28, 29] for which there is no definitive formula and, maybe, no correct answer, just good or bad outcomes.
10 A sense of timing – a refined feel of when to act, aware of the situational realities.
11 Outcomes focused – an ability to understand the futurity of their recommendations and resulting actions.
12 When asked, the ability to successfully assist clients in implementing solutions and building capabilities.

How Organisations Use Consultants

Management consultants are agents of innovative and transformational change, uncertainty managers, and trendsetters [30, 31]. The range of products and services the professional management consultant can provide covers all aspects of an organisation: strategic, financial, operations, human resources, and marketing [3]. It can involve managing the complexities of stakeholder engagement, geographic and product expansion, reimagining supply chains, managing the transition to sustainable production, identifying and managing risk, cyber-security, and much more. It is a challenging vocation but rewarding for those who can establish themselves in a competitive world.

The International Labour Office (ILO) [27] identified five generic consulting purposes that apply across industry sectors, management specialties, and intercession forms (Figure 9).

Figure 9 Generic consulting purposes [Derived from 27, p. 11].

The ILO [27] also described the following ten principal ways organisations use consultants. These roles are not mutually exclusive, often complementary, and can happen within a single project.

1 Providing information

Client reliance on this role has changed as online searching has become the norm. As a result, clients and consultants have access to vast amounts of information, much of which assists organisations in staying up to date with current practices. Consultants often played this role in the past, but technological advances have mitigated that responsibility. However, assisting clients in evaluating fact from fiction remains vital for the professional consultant. New opportunities have also arisen in big data analytics and consultants' ability to provide their clients with information that is not readily available via an online search.

2 Providing specialist resources

Providing information is often an interim or supplementary role to support a client organisation's staff. Here, the consultant has unique skills that are needed for a short time to fill a gap in the business or meet the needs of a particular project. A client might also use the opportunity to bypass new staff hiring restrictions or to limit the budgetary impact of having to keep specialists on the team.

3 Establishing business contacts and linkages

Clients often ask consultants to identify and vet commercial or government contracts to help them fill gaps in the organisation's supply chain; access new markets, new technologies, or funding sources; or identify merger or acquisition targets, especially in sectors or countries where the client has had little prior contact.

4   Providing expert opinion
    This role may be to act as a sounding board for a client or provide a highly specialised opinion on an area where the consultant has particular expertise. In other words, it might be relatively informal or a request for an expert report or testimony.

5   Doing diagnostic work
    Diagnosis is a core role of a professional management consultant. A client will expect the consultant to use various tools to analyse the organisation's internal and external environments. For example, these may include supply chain risks, financial capacity, operational efficacy, skills needs, market image, and growth opportunities. Your role then will be to identify areas for organisational improvement.

6   Developing action proposals
    The development of action proposals and or plans will often follow the diagnosis. At this point, the client may ask the consultant to develop an action plan or seek advice. Alternatives may also be requested, along with recommendations on the best approach.

7   Developing systems and methods
    Developing new systems and methods for a client organisation is an everyday activity for the professional consultant. This role has taken on renewed importance, given significant disruptions to business supply chains induced by the pandemic, the war in Ukraine, and global warming. Changes to systems and methods may follow a diagnosis project and involve any or all areas of an organisation. Typical areas of client concern include information and communications security, operations scheduling, inventory management, human resource planning and remuneration, process integration and control, new technologies, customer interaction, and order processing. The consultant may be asked to undertake one or all activities, from diagnosis, solution identification, and change management to implementation.

8   Planning and managing organisational changes
    Change is a cause of stress and disruption in organisations. As a result, a consultant is often brought in to assist management with the change process, advise on the most appropriate method and approach, oversee the change, encourage those involved, and monitor the changes' effects over time. First, however, a word of warning.
    There is a variation on an old expression that states that an expert is someone from out of town who carries a PowerPoint presentation. While frivolous, organisations sometimes apply that definition to support a controversial position that a client wants to implement. If the client's manager proposes a change likely to receive considerable internal resistance, they may engage an external consultant to put the idea forward. If a consultant suggests the change, it comes from an 'expert.' If the resistance makes subsequent implementation too tricky, or if the change is

unsuccessful, the manager can shift the blame and put the idea down to the wild ravings of the consultant. This management approach by movers within an organisation is a risk for the consultant and should be treated cautiously.

9   Training management and staff
    The training and development of a client's staff is a separate service provided by consultants, often as part of a significant change introduced or sought by the client. For example, it might develop new skills, expand existing capabilities, or improve capacity. General training and management development subjects include leadership, problem-solving, staff training, negotiation, customer relationship building, team development, respect at work, specific technical and process skills development, and workplace health and safety.

10 Counselling and coaching leaders
    The counselling and coaching of managers and entrepreneurs is a trusting relationship between the consultant and their client. It is a personal experience in which a respected consultant can benefit their client through knowledge sharing and behavioural observation in a one-to-one friendly, confidential, and relaxed environment. It has been uncommon for these services to be offered by consultants, although they may be becoming more widespread [32]. Whilst it has been just as rare for counselling and coaching services to be requested by a client [27], where they are provided, the experience can enrich both

So, if a consultant does that, how do they go about it? The next chapter discusses professionalism and details the consulting process from contracting a project until its closure.

3   Becoming a Professional Consultant

> Professionalism is like love: it is made up of the constant flow of little bits of proof that testify to devotion and care. Everything else is pretension or incompetence.
>
> (Tomislav Šola) [33]

The CMC Competency Framework

The word "professional" has several meanings and is dependent on context. In management consulting, the definition chosen is that a professional is "a highly skilled and experienced person who, for gain, does a job that needs special training and a high level of education, and whose performance is characterised by or conforming to the technical and ethical standards of the profession" [34, 35].

There are significant challenges to professionalism: An increasing rate of change, increased competition, more and more accessible substitutes and knowledge sources, technological innovation, and a "growing mistrust of experts" [1]. A client's trust in their advisor and the advisor's competence are the critical ingredients for professional success. So, what is trust?

Maister, Galford, and Green defined trust (T) as credibility (C) plus reliability (R) plus intimacy (I) divided by self-orientation (S), the latter being a measure of the degree to which the professional places their interests ahead of those of their client. Trust has to be earned. "It grows, rather than just appears; it is both rational and emotional, and it is a two-way relationship" [36, p. 28]. Trust in the consultant-client relationship is essential if the advice given is to be taken, no matter how appropriate that advice might be. Beaton summarised that "professionals' motives matter because they are central to trust – and trust is the oil that powers and lubricates not just the professions, but our economy and society" [1, p. 22].

DOI: 10.4324/9781003466987-3

Competence is more challenging to define. White [37, p. 297] defined it simply as "an organism's capacity to interact effectively with its environment." While there are many definitions of competence, in a business context, it is often used to describe a person's ability or capacity to do a job or as an ability to do something successfully or efficiently. The definitions chosen here are that competence measures demonstrated skills, knowledge, and ability. In contrast, competency is the capacity to apply or use those attributes to perform professionally.

To give structure and meaning to the concept of professional competency, in 2014, CMC-Global created a competency framework. In 2022, the framework was updated to include a greater emphasis on technical awareness and skills in communication and diagnostic technology, interpersonal skills (emotional intelligence) and holistic and transformational thinking, and knowledge of the application of social programs such as the UN's 17 sustainability goals [38], ISO's "Guidance on social responsibility" Standard ISO 26000:2010 [39], and anti-bribery provisions. In addition, the 2022 upgrade integrates ISO's "Guidelines for management consultancy services" standard ISO 20700:2017 [40] into the framework [20]. Showing that you meet all competency elements is the foundation of CMC accreditation, while CMC certification is a crucial role of an IMC.

The framework now forms the basis of consultancy excellence and professionalism. It comprises four pillars against which CMCs are assessed (Figure 10):

1　Business insight and aptitude, which includes client specialisation and sectorial knowledge, and consultancy and consulting business insight
2　Practice capabilities, including knowledge and employment of assignment and engagement methodologies and consultative capabilities
3　Consultative behaviour, which includes personal capabilities and conduct
4　Ethic and professional conduct

Accredited IMCs assess each CMC against the 24 areas of required professional competence listed in Figure 11.

A vital pillar of the framework is ethical and professional conduct. Professional management consulting includes a set of moral norms shared and applied by the profession's members. The agreed ICMCI Code of Conduct [41] guides and governs each member through their IMC's ethical and professional behaviour requirements. In turn, individual IMCs have their code covering their members (Appendix D). These codes cover professionalism, sustainability, social responsibility, conflict of interest, and integrity [42] behaviour and expectations in a consulting assignment.

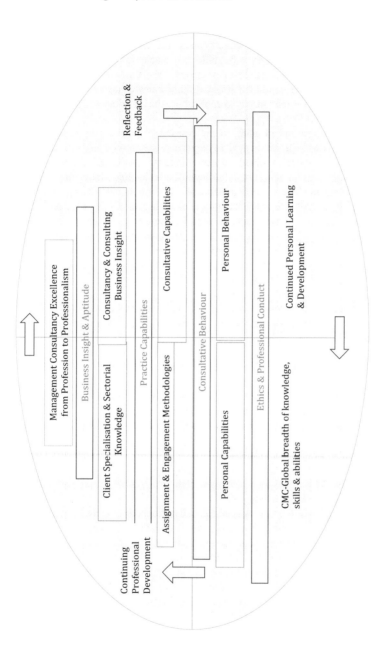

Figure 10 CMC-Global Professional Development and Standards Committee's Competency Framework pillars [20]4F4F. Published with permission.

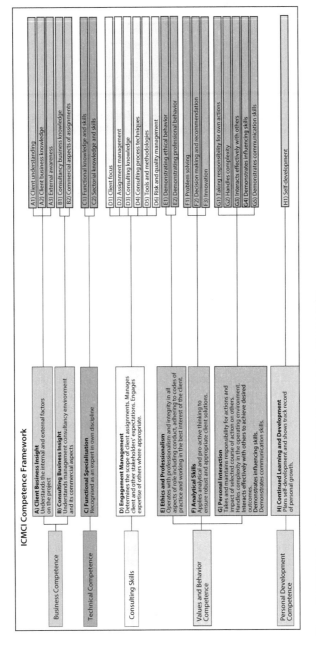

Figure 11 ICMCI Competency Framework 2022 [17]. Published with permission.

Above All, Know Thyself

> The fool doth think he is wise, but the wise man knows himself to be a fool.
>
> *(William Shakespeare, 1564–1616)*

Understanding one's competencies is critical to being a successful consultant. At some point in their career, a client will ask every consultant to conduct a SWOT analysis. But how many have analysed their strengths and weaknesses and sought to identify the opportunities and threats they face? In my experience, few.

Completing a self-SWOT can be emotionally challenging. Yet, the insights gained are fundamental to understanding the value a consultant can and cannot add to their client's businesses. It is also essential to grasp what additional skills will be required to succeed professionally. The key to a successful SWOT analysis is identifying each strength and weakness and questioning its relevance. Asking "So what?" is just as important as answering the questions, "What are my strengths?" and "What are my weaknesses?" Once identified, weaknesses can be bolstered by additional learning or by identifying and partnering with those whose areas of strength complement fields of weakness.

Also, it is essential to understand your preferred temperament and how it fits with others. A commonly used tool to analyse character is the Myers-Briggs Type Indicator® instrument [43]. Another similar tool is the Keirsey Temperament Sorter [44]. Both tests are based on the work in the 1940s of psychologist Carl Jung and are used by many consultants and psychologists focused on team building and dynamics. Finally, a sometimes preferred test is the Birkman 4 Quadrant Personality Test, designed to assess interests, behaviours, stress management, and organisational abilities [45]. Whichever one you use (you could try all three), completing a psychological profile will help you to understand your behaviours and those for and with whom you work and live.

Be PESTEL Aware

As well as having insight into their competencies, professional consultants must be deeply aware of the political, economic, sociocultural, technological, environmental, and legal (PESTEL) impacts on their clients. Earth is a complex place. Remaining aware and objective is increasingly difficult as access to information becomes more available and accessible. Filtering that information for what is 'real' and what is 'fake' is more complicated. Nevertheless, professionals must strive to sort the data wheat from the chaff and then understand the impacts and implications of the realities for themselves and their clients, all while maintaining objectivity.

A key here is to validate, or fact check, all data found. Far too much data trash is floating around the internet to accept information as factual without first checking it for truthfulness, accuracy, and relevance. Use only credible sources; those you know have a high probability of being repositories of credible information. Then, check each piece of information against another trustworthy source. Ignore the rest.

Be Industry Aware

For the professional consultant, developing a profound grasp of the PESTEL forces impacting a client's business applies equally to understanding the industry or industries in which they operate. More than forty years ago, Harvard luminary Professor Michael Porter isolated five distinct forces determining each sector's competitiveness level. As a guide to choosing the nature and level of competition in an industry, *Porter's 5 Forces Analysis* [46] remains a valuable starting point.

Four of the five forces work to regulate the intensity of rivalry in any particular industry. For example, how easy it is for new entrants to enter, how hard it is for existing players to leave, how great, suitable, and accessible substitute products are, and how much power suppliers and buyers have. The intensity of rivalry puts downward pressure on prices, reducing industry profitability. Professional consultants must understand this in terms of their industry and have a deep awareness of the state of their clients' industries if they are to be effective.

Learn to Recognise Relationships

Businesses are, at their most basic level, simple organisms. Each is an interconnected system consisting of different functional components encompassing marketing, financial control, operations, and human resources, all bound together by management within an industry and complex macro-environment (Figure 12). They are like Venn diagrams with an ecosystem of different actors. Yet, every business is unique and complex because each comprises a distinctive combination of the knowledge, skills, and attributes of those who encompass the human resources component of the organisation and the internal and external linkages and systems they form. This uniqueness holds irrespective of business type, although some might focus more on one element than another and vary their structure accordingly. The larger the organisation's number employed, the more intricate the combination of relationships becomes. A business is that simple and that complex.

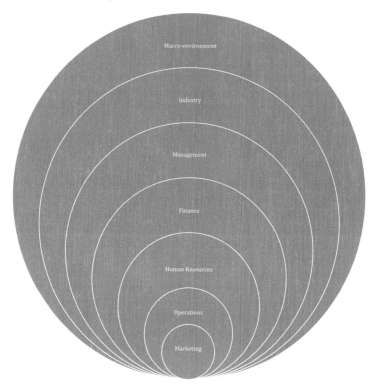

Figure 12 The basic structure of a business and its macro and industry environment.

Therefore, identifying relationships is fundamental to a management consultant understanding their client's business. Whether consultants perceive themselves as specialists or generalists doesn't matter. Both types must seek to understand the relationships affected by consulting project intervention.

So, how does one gain an in-depth understanding of such an organism within the typically short time available for a professional management consulting project?

4 Thinking Critically to Effect and Manage Change

> Alice laughed: "There's no use trying," she said; "one can't believe impossible things." "I daresay you haven't had much practice," said the Queen. "When I was younger, I always did it for half an hour a day. Why, sometimes, I've believed as many as six impossible things before breakfast."
>
> (Lewis Carroll, 1865)

Think Critically to Gain Understanding

The answer to how to gain an in-depth understanding lies in viewing the organisation as an interconnected system, undertaking careful research, and using simple, tried, and tested models. Unfortunately, consultants often have to work in an ambiguous grey zone, in which there is no black or white answer, and seek solutions to what Rittel and Webber called "wicked problems" [28]: problems that are essentially unique and which have no right or wrong answers, just good or bad outcomes.

Consultants must be ready to advise their clients on the available options and guide them through the necessary changes and risk mitigation steps. As we have seen recently, some of those changes will be sudden and dramatic, as has been the case in response to the COVID-19 pandemic. So-called "black swan" events, like a pandemic, have a small probability of happening and are unpredictable [47], but their impacts are sometimes profound. Others will be longer-term, allowing solutions to be planned and effects mitigated.

Understanding the technology surrounding environmentally friendly product manufacture and its potential impacts on manufacturing, the economy, workforce requirements, and society will be essential for those professional consultants seeking to position their clients for a net zero carbon economy. So will the need to pinpoint where and what changes will be required for clients to take full advantage of the changing landscape and minimise the impacts

DOI: 10.4324/9781003466987-4

when risks become a reality. Clients are looking for solutions and are typically risk-averse. Despite that, a 2019 global study of eight thousand senior executives found that the two most important attributes they sought "when deciding which consulting firm to hire" were an "innovative approach" and the methodologies used by the firm [48, p. 3].

Consultants knowing more than senior employees in a client's business are rare. The key is correctly asking the right people the appropriate, challenging questions and then learning to process the information and produce meaningful, helpful output. A crucial element of each consultancy practice is the individual consultants' ability to think critically and creatively. So what exactly is "critical and creative thinking," and what steps are required?

The Australian Curriculum [49] describes it this way, in part:

> Critical and creative thinking involves … thinking broadly and deeply using skills, behaviours and dispositions such as reason, logic, resourcefulness, imagination and innovation in all learning areas …. Thinking that is productive, purposeful and intentional is at the centre of effective learning" (Figure 13).

While your knowledge and experiences can streamline this process, they can also act as a block to thinking in new ways and seeking novel solutions.

With practice, by applying a thinking skills system, individuals can understand the processes to combat problems, unfamiliar information, and new ideas. This approach is vital to effective consulting.

Critical and creative thinking involves an eight-step process (Figure 14):

1 Understanding the problem
2 Exploring its boundaries
3 Questioning assumptions
4 Imagining new perspectives
5 Identifying weaknesses
6 Justifying a solution
7 Acknowledging limitations
8 Reflecting on alternatives

Critical and creative thinking must become second nature for the professional consultant and is at the heart of your ability to innovate. It's what you are paid to do. When the drama becomes a reality, time will be of the essence. Thinking critically and creatively must be intuitive when that happens. Now is the time to practise so that your clients can pivot quickly and achieve optimal outcomes when that time comes.

UNDERSTAND THE RELATIONSHIPS

The American philosopher and writer Aldous Huxley identified that knowledge is acquired when we fit a new experience into concepts based on

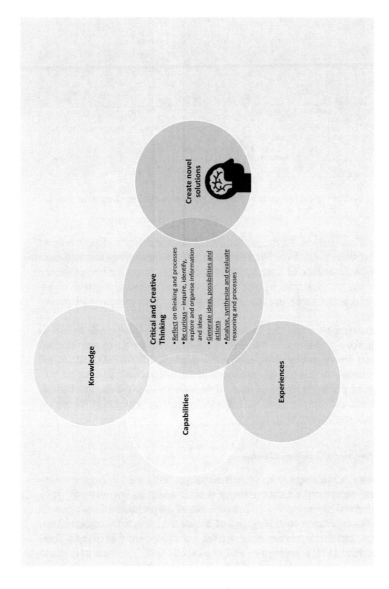

Figure 13 Critical and creative thinking process to create novel solutions [49].

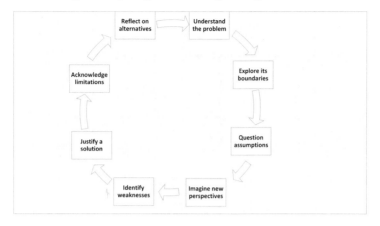

Figure 14 The critical and creative thinking process. Australian Curriculum (Version 8.4), 2023.

our old experiences. As the simplicity and complexity of a client's internal and external relationships become understood, the knowledge acquired from past experiences can be brought to bear to develop solutions to new problems. However, knowing who will be the beneficiaries and who might be disadvantaged before achieving that outcome is essential to ensure future project success.

Management consulting is a cumulative process. It's been described as being like a pinball game. You win one game, and you get to play another. It's also a very competitive industry. For example, IBISWorld (2020) found some seventy-two thousand consultants in Australia alone![1] To compete successfully, a consultant must understand the technicalities of their expertise and the depth and complexity of their client's internal and external relationships. When in doubt, seek help.

Leading and Managing Change

"Change management is an organisational process aimed at helping stakeholders accept and embrace changes in their operating environment" [50]. Leading and managing change is a core role of the professional management consultant. Often, a consulting project becomes a catalyst for organisational change, and the consultant must oversee and implement that change. Transition impacts all organisations and at all levels [51]. Yet, most attempts to transform an organisation fail [52]. So, what are the steps?

While several models are available to guide you with implementation, one commonly used is Kotter's eight-step process for leading change [53] (Figure 15).

Create	Create a sense of urgency
Build	Build a guiding coalition
Form	Form a strategic vision and initiatives
Enlist	Enlist a volunteer army
Enable	Enable action by removing barriers
Generate	Generate short-term wins
Sustain	Sustain acceleration
Institute	Institute change

Figure 15 Kotter's eight-step process for managing change.

Kotter's approach focuses on combining leadership and management, with leadership facilitating management processes to create a vision for change, energise action, inspire innovation, and promote celebration. The process involves uncovering untapped leadership at all levels of the organisation to make change happen.

Of course, change implementation will only be successful with the support of those in the organisation. Hiatt's ADKAR model [54] for understanding the phases of change at the individual level is helpful. Hiatt identified the following five stages of change for employees:

1   Awareness of the individual of the need for change
2   Desire for change
3   Knowledge of the change process
4   The ability of the individual to implement the change needed
5   Reinforcement of the individual to ensure the sustainability of the benefits of change

The United States Agency for International Development (USAID) has promoted a seven-step process as "best practice" [50]. In short:

1   Establish a vision with which staff identifies
2   Involve senior leadership and gain their commitment and involvement
3   Develop a change management plan

4   Engage stakeholders
5   Communicate at all levels
6   Create infrastructure to support the adoption
7   Measure progress

The impact of change in an organisation can be broad or restricted to a specific business area. However, all changes will have an effect. As stated, each organisation is a complex web of interconnected systems: you pick a flower in one, and you change all. Therefore, the outcomes must be fully understood at the beginning of the process. That means planning. Essential components of a change management plan recommended by USAID include [50, p. 4]:

1   *Vision and goals*
2   *Stakeholders*
3   *Resources*
4   *Time-specific milestones*
5   *Communication tools and strategy, including key messages*
6   *Metrics*
7   *Roles and responsibilities*
8   *Results from change readiness or risk analysis (if applicable)*

Remember, the plan doesn't need to be long; it just needs to be thorough, clear, and achievable.

Although involving all stakeholders from the outset is essential in most instances, and bottom-up change is likely to be better tolerated than when implemented from the top, practicality means that a top-down approach might sometimes be necessary [50]. In summary, successful change requires a clear-cut need and awareness of that need, a clearly stated vision for the desired change outcomes, a sense of urgency, a structured process for implementing change, and the ability and willingness of those effecting change to execute it well. Implementing change necessitates close cooperation between lead clients and the consultant if it is to be successful and owned by those affected. It is not a job for the consultant alone. Collaboration with members of Change Management Institutes[2] or the Association of Change Management Professionals[3] can also be beneficial.

Figure 16 summarises the planning steps for successfully leading and managing organisational change.

Additional Essential Skills Every Professional Consultant Must Master

Many skills and tools are needed to help consultants understand their and clients' situations. Which you favour will depend on the type of consultant you are and want to be and your skillset. Others are more generic, like

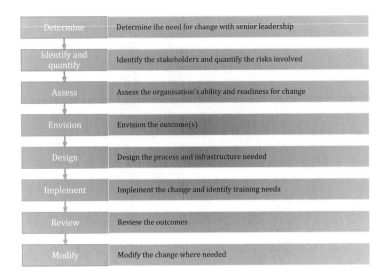

Determine	Determine the need for change with senior leadership
Identify and quantify	Identify the stakeholders and quantify the risks involved
Assess	Assess the organisation's ability and readiness for change
Envision	Envision the outcome(s)
Design	Design the process and infrastructure needed
Implement	Implement the change and identify training needs
Review	Review the outcomes
Modify	Modify the change where needed

Figure 16 The planning steps for leading and managing organisational change.

those discussed already. However, there are more skills that every consultant, whether a specialist or generalist, must master for their and their client's benefit.

1   Know how to read and analyse a financial report. Much can be learnt from a glance at a balance sheet and income statement. For example, how liquid is the business, how much stock is held, how much debt is being carried, how quickly are payments from customers being made, and how profitable is the organisation compared to others in its sector? For public companies, interpreting the annual report is essential if you have to come to grips with not just what has been stated but often with what has remained unsaid. You will usually need to use your forensic skills to determine the root causes of the issues faced by a client. Your forensic skills will also be required to determine the risk profile for privately held businesses. You must learn to use and interpret key accounting ratios for these purposes.

A list of common financial ratios can be found in Appendix F. However, a valuable tool to help interpret the relationship between an income statement and a balance sheet is the DuPont model for analysing return on equity (ROE), shown in Figure 17.

2   Truth-seeking is a skill cherished by the best consultants. Learn to listen, not just to the words but to the message, and to ask questions. It's often not what people say but what they don't say that's important. Picking up on the

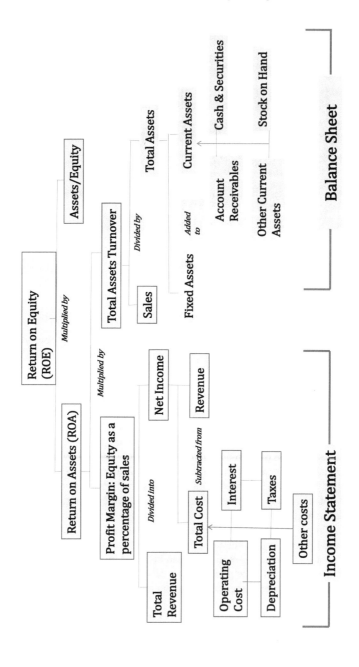

Figure 17 The DuPont analysis model for calculating return on equity.

clues being given verbally and from body language will help you gain the more profound understanding needed to grasp the issues at hand fully.

3   Develop and practise your questioning skills.

4   For your business survival:

    a   Know your positioning strategy. How are you different from other competing consultants? Why would a client select you as a consultant? How can your skills complement those of other consultants? Explore how your knowledge, skills, and attributes might fit with other consultants.

    b   Determine your product, sector, geographic scope, and growth rate. With too narrow a focus, if that area changes or disappears, so will your business. However, maintaining service quality and resourcing become much more challenging with too broad a focus. These are some of the business choices that you must make.

    c   Always know how much money you have available and where your future funds will come from. All businesses, including consultancies, can lose money, at least for a while, but the survivors don't have to fold. Why? Because they continue to have access to cash. Always ensure you can access sufficient money to support yourself and your business.

You are now prepared to start consulting and establishing a client relationship. That's when the fun begins!

Notes

1 The IBISWorld estimate of the number of consultants is thought to be too high. For example, an analysis by this author of the Australian Business Register in June 2022 found 29,189 individual registrations for "Management and Related Advisory Services," whereas, in February 2022, IBISWorld reported that the industry consisted of 89,668 businesses.

2 Change Management Institute - For Change Professionals (change-management-institute.com).

3 Association of Change Management Professionals (acmpglobal.org).

5 The Consulting Process – Preparation and Contracting

> Successful organisations understand the importance of implementation, not just strategy, and, moreover, recognise the crucial role of their people in this process.
>
> (Jeffrey Pfeffer) [55]

Preparing for the First Meeting

Rule #1: Be prepared! Please don't go to a potential or existing client without prior knowledge of what they do, who they serve, and the industry in which they work. A consultant must first gain a deep understanding of their client and its industry. Remember, the first impression will endure, and there is only one opportunity to make an outstanding first impression. Creating that impression starts with your Google and LinkedIn profiles. Your client will likely have reviewed those before their first meeting with you.

Step 1: Gain a broad understanding of the business. First, look at the client as a system. Next, conduct a comprehensive review of the client's website and, if published, any annual or other company reports—finally, research news reports, industry reports, such as Source Global Research, customer ratings, and comments. Prepare informed questions to ask at the first meeting; this will show you have done your homework.

Step 2: Study the industry. What are the current issues facing the industry as a whole? Analyse the political, economic, sociocultural, technological, environmental, and legal environments. What is the nature of competition in the industry? Although it's more than forty years since Porter developed his "Five Forces Model" [46], it remains a valuable tool when considering the nature of an industry's competitiveness and supply chain complexities (*Figure 18*). Finally, consider your client's fit in terms of its strategic position and the levels of uncertainty and difficulty it faces.

Step 3: Prepare some initial questions. Base these on your research and use a logical sequence. For example, the 5Ws plus 1 is useful: Why is the consultancy

DOI: 10.4324/9781003466987-5

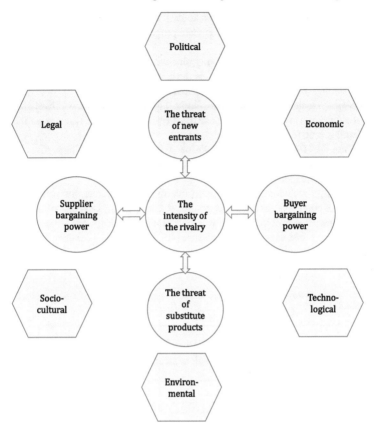

Figure 18 The PESTEL and Porter's five industry forces impacting business and industry rivalry.

needed? What will be required? Who will be affected? Where will the consultancy take place? When is it required? How does the client see it happening? Asking informed questions can help build a relationship with your client.

At the First Meeting

Step 4: Actively listen to what your client has to say. Careful listening is the basis of skilful questioning. What are the critical relationships and intraorganisational conflicts? Within the client organisation, who has the main interest in the success or failure of the project? Who are the change leaders, and who has a stake in the work's success? Who will be the prominent supporters? Who may be opposed? Who are the stakeholders that need to be involved? Who needs to be at the table as the assignment progresses? What will a successful project look like?

Step 5: Clarify expectations. Determine the engagement terms and conditions for the project. Be sure to define the consultancy's objectives, deliverables, timing, roles and responsibilities, and fees and expenses.

Step 6: Document what has been learnt. This documentation will likely be in the form of a proposal to undertake a project. However, it is also a potential referral source for future work.

Rule #2: Don't attempt to take on a job outside your expertise. If needed, call in other experts to work with you or leave the work to others with more specific experience.

Although each consultant is responsible for their resources and work, the client is accountable for decisions, results, outputs, and impacts on stakeholders. Figure 19 shows that the consulting process includes three primary actions: contracting, execution, and closure [40]. In addition, it contains a list of CMC-Global's policies that direct the process.

The following sections describe each step in detail.

Contracting

> Successful negotiation is not about getting to 'yes'; it's about mastering 'no' and understanding the path to an agreement [57].

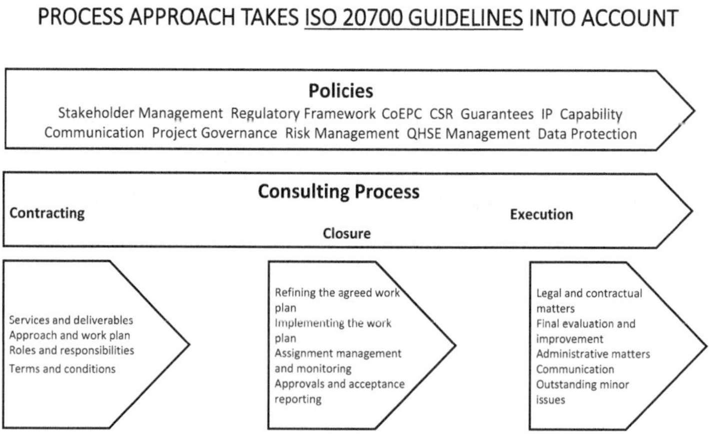

PROCESS APPROACH TAKES ISO 20700 GUIDELINES INTO ACCOUNT

Figure 19 The typical consulting process, taking ISO 20700:2017 into account [20, 40, 56]. Published with permission.

Contracting aims to develop and achieve mutual understanding and agreement between the consultant and client on the services provided. The resulting contract should protect the interests of both parties. It involves defining and agreeing on six key elements:

1 Context
2 Services to be provided and the deliverables expected
3 The consultant's approach and work plan
4 The roles and responsibilities of each party
5 Acceptance criteria
6 Contract terms and conditions

While there are many sources of information for the contracting phase, the consultant must determine their client's professed needs and expectations for the project early on, identify all stakeholders who might be impacted, and detect the potential constraints and risks involved. Asking the right questions at the outset is crucial for informing these needs and expectations.

The consultant will need to progress through these elements for each assignment. This requirement will apply whether or not the work is part of a longer-term project with an existing client.

The Context

Appreciating the context in which the assignment occurs is critical to completing a successful consulting project. This step involves gathering background information on the organisation and its environment and determining client and stakeholder assumptions, project scope, constraints, and risks.

Risk and Quality Management

We all work in a volatile, uncertain, complex, and ambiguous world. Managing client risk is a core activity of the professional management consultant. As a result, individual consultants must "continually anticipate, evaluate, prioritise and manage risks and quality issues associated with (each) assignment" [40, p. 9]. The provision of objective advice will often necessitate the consultant having to manage a variety of possible conflicts.

The assessment of risk requires a disciplined approach. One such approach is Boyd's 1974 OODA loop, which suggests a recurrent observation, orientation, decision-making, and action cycle. This method follows the action learning cycle (Learn, Plan, Act, Reflect) and the scientific method of hypothesis development (Hypothesise, Test, Analyse, Report) approaches. OODA has become a common but not universally accepted way to evaluate and manage uncertainty. However, whatever method is used, the consultant must remain aware of the risks to an assignment, thereby to themselves and their reputation.

A sound practice is completing a risk assessment before starting a project. Work closely with your client and other stakeholders, and consider risks from goal variances within your and the client's teams. If the assignment goals are not agreed upon, the project is at risk of failure. Using a risk-assessment template will structure your assessment and allow for the probability and impact of each risk to be quantified, monitored, and reported. Tables 2 and 3 offer some simple headings for your risk management template:

Once you have created your risk assessment table, rank the risks by risk score. The risks can then be monitored, mitigation actions taken, modified, or deleted as the assignment progresses or risk factors change. For example:

Managing client and assignment risks is part of the job, but the need for a consultant to manage their own risk cannot be ignored. A critical risk is a conflict of interest. Such conflicts might stem from previous or current client relationships, family, dealings with other consultants, financial, legal, or regulatory restrictions, or other personal and business relationships. In many cases, the consultant can manage conflicts by disclosing relationships that might cause a conflict of interest and by seeking written approval to proceed from affected stakeholders. Alternatively, disputes might be governed effectively by formal non-disclosure or other agreements. Table 4 lists principal risk sources, the factors to consider, and mitigation methods, while Table 5 lists familiar sources of conflict of interest.

Table 2 Risk assessment template headings

Risk	Probability of occurrence (0–1, where one is certain	Who will be impacted	Impact score (0–10, where 10 is the maximum impact	Risk score/10 (Prob. × Imp)	Mitigate

Table 3 Risk assessment example

Risk	Probability of occurrence (0–1, where one is certain	Who will be impacted	Impact score (0–10, where 10 is the maximum impact	Risk score/10 (Prob. × Imp)	Mitigate
Pandemic	1.0	Everyone	10	10	Vaccine development and administration Mask wearing Quarantine

Table 4 IMC Australia's risk identification for professional management consultants [cited in 40, p. 27]

Principal sources of risk	Factors to consider	Mitigation
Client: Does the client or its management team pose issues that could affect the successful completion of the assignment?	Past dealings with the organisation and its principles. Any reputational or integrity concerns related to the prospective client, its principles, or its industry. A financial consideration could impair the client's ability to pay the consultant.	Ensure that the client makes available all necessary resources. Financial concerns can be reduced by negotiating payment arrangements, such as advances or milestone payments. Be prepared to decline to work for a prospective client if you have serious concerns.
Nature of engagement: Does the heart of the particular assignment pose additional risks to successful completion?	Public profile, sensitivity, and controversy around issues to be examined. Significant recent changes at the client. Any requirements to deviate from the consultant's usual policies and procedures. Client's project governance and availability of client data.	Seek clarity of project governance and data sources in advance. You should be prepared to decline a particular assignment if you have serious concerns.
Quality of delivery: Are there risks in the consultant's ability to oversee and deliver the project to the client's satisfaction and without risk to the consultant's reputation?	Existence of consultant's experience with methodologies deployed in the assignment. Availability of consultancy staff with the skills and experience to conduct the engagement. Sufficient budget to execute the project to a high standard.	A functioning quality management program. Have a more senior, experienced management consultant supervise and approve your analysis and recommendations. Independent internal review. Take care in the precise wording of your findings and recommendations. Place restrictions on the distribution or reliance upon your report.
Reputation: Is there a risk to your or your firm's reputation associated with the client, the industry, or the project?	Check any legal requirements. Also, consider your and your firm's ethical framework, cultural mores, and societal expectations.	Complete a due diligence assessment of the client by reviewing news sources, court findings, and police records. Monitor social and legislative trends.

All decisions relating to client and engagement risks and risk mitigation strategies should be approved and documented at a senior level according to the consultant's policies and procedures.

Table 5 IMC Australia's potential sources of conflict of interest [cited by 40, p. 23].

Source	Explanation
Multiple projects with the same client at a different level or different location	Are there parallel or similar contracts in the same group, past or present?
The client is a former client.	Where a client is also a former client, has the consultant provided previous advice or conducted an earlier analysis that would constrain the consultant's direction in the new situation?
The consultant has a client or a former client in the same industry	Where the consultant has a current or former client, perhaps in the same industry as the client that they now seek to advise, does the consultant have proprietary information that could impact their advice?
Staff members have a relationship.	Do any staff members at the consulting firm have family relationships with client staff members, particularly those in management positions?
Internal consulting organisations	Do any staff members at the consulting firm have hierarchical relationships with the client or recipient staff members, particularly those in management positions?
The consultant or staff have a financial interest.	Does the consulting firm or its staff members have a financial interest in the client or any of its management team members, including an overdue account receivable, loan or equity investment?
The consultant has an audit relationship with the client	Where the consultant also has a financial audit relationship with the client, are the prospective consulting services allowed by the relevant securities regulator? Note that where a client is also an audit client but not subject to securities regulation, the client's audit committee may choose to restrict the additional services that the consultant may provide as a matter of policy.
Other	Other business relationships may include situations where the consulting firm or its staff share a client's interest in a third-party contract (such as a software partnership, leased premises, a subscription to sports tickets, etc.) Alternatively, where the consulting firm or its staff members are "captive" to the staff of the client, as in the case of "contract" or "interim" management or "internal consultants".

Defining the Services and Deliverables

There are three main ways that a client will request consultants to propose and present for a job:

1 Open tender request
2 Request for a quotation (RFQ), for a proposal (RFP), or to tender for a project
3 Request for an Expression of Interest (EOI)

Government agencies often employ the first method to determine the skills and experience available for a significant or complex project. An open tender process usually takes time from request to agreement.

The second method is more limited in its targets. In this case, a request might be sent to one or just a few consultants, often from a client to a consultant they have worked with successfully before or one favourably referred. Usually, the targeted consultants have already undergone a pre-approval process, such as a panel selection. Such an approach is not constrained by legislation or internal regulations prohibiting awarding consulting contracts without an open or selective tender process. An RFQ will typically include information about the client, a brief description of the issues, budget and timetable constraints, and contact information, including a proposal deadline. It is worth noting that consulting team members for Federal Government consulting projects may require a pre-approved security clearance.

An EOI usually leads to an RFP and involves a two-step process where a proposal is the second step. First, it is often used to determine a shortlist of qualified consultants to move to the second step by their experience, subject or industry knowledge, and other client-specific terms. Typically, the EOI presents an overview of the issues at hand and asks consultants to explain how their qualifications make them eligible and what strategies they might use or have used in other cases to deal with a similar issue. The resulting shortlist is then invited to submit a formal proposal.

An RFP, or RFQ, is very similar in content to a Terms of Reference (TOR) – and in instances where a TOR has been developed, it is usually provided as part of an open tender request or RFQ.

Although the client selects a sole qualified consulting firm and directly negotiates a legal contract in some situations, the agreement process is very similar to developing a formal proposal. The contract must include a complete description of the provided services, the expected outcomes, and the required deliverables. How the services will be evaluated and the conditions and process for client acceptance of the project outcomes should also be explained. In a work plan, clearly describe the project's objectives, scope and expectations, and the consultant's approach and proposed methodology.

The work plan might take any one of a variety of forms. For example, a Gantt chart can graphically describe the project steps, timetable and milestones, resource allocation, and budget. Another method is to provide a simple table with that information.

In preparation for an assignment, the client will often prepare a TOR, which they will send out in their call for consulting proposals. A TOR usually includes a preliminary problem statement and may have been developed internally or by another consultant. You should know how the TOR was designed and consider whether it is practical or achievable. Requesting an interview to discuss the assignment with a client is advised.

Typically, a TOR will include [27, p. 167]

- *A description of the problem(s) to be solved*
- *Objectives and expected results of the assignment (i.e. what is to be achieved, knowledge transfer, capacity-building, and deliverables)*
- *Background and supporting information (on the client organisation, stakeholders, related projects, and consultancies, past efforts to solve problems, etc.)*
- *Budget estimate or resource limit*
- *Timetable (start and completion dates, key stages, and control dates)*
- *Interim and final reporting (dates, form, number of copies, whom, etc.)*
- *Inputs to be provided by the client (further information and documentation, staff time, secretarial support, transport, etc.)*
- *Exclusions from the assignment (what will not be its object)*
- *Constraints and other factors likely to affect the project*
- *Profile and competencies of eligible consultants*
- *Contact persons and addresses and communication channels*

Sometimes, a client will not issue a TOR but prefers to select a consultant based on prior experience or a trusted referral. In such a case, the client will likely discuss the project with the chosen consultant and confirm the assignment by accepting a proposal.

Consultant's Approach and Workplan

Following a client's approach, either directly or indirectly, it is usual for the consultant to prepare a proposal to undertake the work described in the client's request. This preparation will necessitate paying close attention to any weighting criteria detailed in the TOR or RFQ.

Proposal development

The lead consultant begins by designing strategy and planning tasks in developing a proposal. Strategic issues are about the consulting approach to be taken. Much of the approach will define each consultant's resource use and process role. The following are also components of the strategic reckoning:

- How is the assignment going to be organised?
    - How will consultants be introduced to the organisation?
    - What expectations of cooperation does the consultant have?
    - Who will do what to ensure the assignment moves in an orderly way?
- Which stakeholders are going to be involved and impacted?
- What activities must the consultants complete, and what are the client's responsibilities?
- Which client documents and data will be available, and who will be the client's point of contact for those?

- What team meetings, projects and other forms of group work will be used, and who will be involved?
- Will special training and information activities be necessary?
- How will roles shift as the consulting assignment progresses?

Based on the strategy, the consultant can then outline the assignment plan. Essential elements of planning include the following:

- A Statement of Objectives – Each objective should be specific, measurable, achievable, realistic, and timed (SMART). Then, using the data collected, describe the problem and outline the goals to be achieved, defining the benefits to the client.
- Specific deliverables – As the project moves through each phase, indicate the outcome and deliverables for each step to the client.
- Timing – The estimated timing of each phase and deliverable should be clearly stated. The overall assignment timing depends on the client's needs, tempered with the availability of both client and consultant resources and the reality of the scale of change taking place.
- Roles and Responsibilities
- A preliminary calculation of the fees and expenses associated with delivering the service.

Preparing Proposals

With the strategy and an assignment plan outlined, the next step is to write a formal proposal. Proposals are essential selling documents – the client has not yet decided [27], and they allow you to sell the firm's consulting services. Therefore, although you may have a vision of how to solve the client's problem(s) successfully, that vision must be communicated clearly in writing. It's also important to note that a successful proposal will become the basis of a formal agreement, so great care is needed with its drafting.

A professional proposal is usually organised around the following eight headings:

1 Executive summary – limit this to one page. It should just be a summary of the salient points from your proposal.
2 Introduction – include a statement of interest in the assignment, thank the client for the opportunity to propose, and provide a brief overview of how the proposal is organised.
3 Background – include an overview of the client's situation or specific assignment context, including a clear statement defining the issue(s) and the purpose and objectives of the assignment.
4 Project scope and methodology – this is also called the 'engagement' [27] section. It is the time to introduce the chosen strategic consulting approach,

define what is in and out of scope, outline the work plan, and identify deliverables or milestones. For example, describe any assignment assumptions, what will be produced, when and if staff allocation has been completed, and by whom. For instance, identify which staff resources, office space, equipment, and other resources are to be provided by each party.

5   Outcomes, services, and deliverables – include a clear statement that outlines the expected results, services to be offered, and what deliverables will be provided. The provision of each deliverable will often be linked to your fee schedule. Of course, this will vary from project to project and may well be specified by your client, so your need to be flexible should be anticipated.

6   Qualifications and experience – outline these for the firm and the individual(s) assigned to carry out the assignment and include each consultant's name, qualifications, relevant experiences, and job role(s). The roles and responsibilities of the consultant, client, and stakeholders should form part of the agreement. The resulting contract should also describe all data, information, and technological resources to be supplied and required for the job.

As well as addressing each item in the TOR or RFQ, you will need to specify in your proposal how the project will be managed; in particular, to identify the project leader and the decision-making, direction, risk mitigation, and quality control processes to be employed. In addition, the agreement should describe the project evaluation process and state the measurable milestones to be achieved and how the milestones will be reported.

Professional fees and expenses – this section details the specific prices for the staff and roles defined in Section 6. The client's TOR or RFQ may require detailed cost and time allocations for each individual involved in the project. Where specific fees cannot be provided for a phase of the assignment – for example, when prices cannot be estimated before the diagnosis and development of solutions to the identified problems – be sure to state that clearly. Relate expenses directly to the methodology laid out in the proposal. You should also note the standard terms of payment – traditionally linked to milestones or deliverables. You should also know that many government panels have pre-agreed payment amounts for different consultant levels.

Engagement conditions and terms – This is where the sundry issues are compiled. For example, how to record and notify changes in scope, contracting terms by either party, ownership of copyright or other intellectual property rights, the applicability of and adherence to relevant codes of professional conduct and ethics, liability issues, how termination may occur, and how to handle dispute and arbitration matters.

Conclusion – Specify acceptance criteria and detail key performance indicators and project milestones. End with a brief statement thanking the client, inviting them to contact a specific person if they have any questions about the proposal, and encouraging them to engage in conversation to clarify any missed expectations or misstated terms or conditions. Lastly, provide information on how proposal follow-up and acceptance occur.

These headings may vary from business to business, but the general thrust of the information needed is the same. There are also alternative options to a full formal proposal. They include a Letter of Understanding (LOU), a Letter of Engagement (LOE), and a Letter of Agreement (LOA). These three letters provide the required information under the IMC "Code of Professional Conduct and Ethics," discussed later in Chapter 8.

Getting the agreement right is essential for both parties, but it will be in its execution when 'the rubber hits the road': that is the test.

6 The Consulting Process – Execution and Closure Execution

> Ideas don't make you rich. The correct execution of ideas does.
>
> (Felix Dennis, 2006) [58]

"Execution is the performance of the services agreed upon in the contracting phase" [40, p. 12]. In this stage, what has been approved is delivered. Therefore, it cannot start until an agreement has been reached and the contracting phase is completed. Outcomes should include providing the agreed-upon services and deliverables, recommendations and future approaches, and ongoing evaluation and improvement suggestions. Typical steps include the following:

1 Refinement of the agreed work plan detail. This work must be done closely with your client to ensure approval, followed by work plan implementation. Preparation will include gathering and analysing pertinent data, reviewing business models and past practices, and summarising the issues. When considering change, there are six essential questions a consultant needs to ask and answer. The responses will come from a situation assessment and a discussion with your client and other stakeholders. Beware of unfounded assumptions; they can lead to misdirection and humiliation for a consultant. Instead, base your analysis on your research.

1 Why will it happen?
2 What will be required?
3 Who will be affected?
4 When should and can it happen?
5 Where will it happen?
6 How will it happen?

2 Options analyses – to identify and evaluate the alternative actions available to address each issue and then shortlist the most appropriate

a Making recommendations on which options to adopt and providing an implementation plan and summary of expected outcomes

DOI: 10.4324/9781003466987-6

b   Presentation of your suggestions to the client and or stakeholders and obtaining client acceptance of those recommendations

c   Implementation – including the execution of the accepted recommendations, monitoring progress, and outcomes evaluation

3   Assignment management and monitoring

The key to a successful assignment is for the consultant, client, and affected stakeholders to collaborate to ensure effective project coordination. Within the context of the agreement, each of the following elements should be considered to achieve success:

a   Project governance is a client's responsibility, and final decisions rest with them. Any disagreements must be handled per the terms of the agreement.

b   Project management – the consultant is responsible for ensuring the effective and efficient carriage of the assignment.

c   Resource management – resources specified in the agreement should be available and managed as agreed. The lead consultant ensures that all involved in the project have the necessary experience, skills, and consulting competencies.

d   A commitment of resources – the consultant is responsible for the allocation and deployment of consulting resources and for liaising with their clients and stakeholders to ensure that work is coordinated, effective, and efficient.

e   Monitoring progress and change control is a formal process, a central element of effective document control and management.[1] The professional consultant will have a change control system to deal with significant changes in an assignment. These might be from deviations in the agreed work plan, a shift in context, changes in the operating environment, consulting team, or client expectations. If sufficiently significant, changes may necessitate a renegotiation of the agreement.

f   Risk and quality management – parties must follow the agreed risk and quality management methodologies.

g   Communication and reporting should be defined and agreed to during the contracting phase. A suggested approach is to specify the following:

i   How will reporting and communication be done (i.e. in person, in writing, by email, etc.)?

ii   When and how often will reporting be expected?

iii Where will reports and communications be sent and kept?

iv   Who will be responsible for reporting and initiating communications, and to whom?

v   Why will reports and communications be initiated (i.e. what will be the triggers for creating a writing or communication)?

vi   What will be the structure of a report?

h   Evaluation and feedback – ideally, this will be ongoing throughout the assignment. Regular meetings between the consultant and client are essential to ensure project progress stays on track and prompt variations can be made whenever needed. While this process is likely structured, building a formal evaluation process into the assignment is good practice. Use a neutral third party to evaluate to encourage a frank assessment of the project's outcomes and resources.

i   Assignment approvals and acceptance – as with each other part of the assignment, this should be a pre-agreed process that includes the commercial implications of acceptance or rejection—more on this in the following section, Closure.

Closure

> I was bitterly resentful but somehow greatly relieved. And I respected him enormously for his clarity of thought, his obvious caring, and his unwillingness to equivocate in delivering bad news.
>
> (Kay Redfield Jamison, 2015) [59].

Closure aims to bring an orderly end to the consultancy. This stage is as crucial to the consulting process as Contracting and Execution. However, there is occasionally a temptation to rush project closure or to brush it off as unimportant; that would be a mistake. The closure is your last chance to finalise legal and contractual matters, evaluate your project's successes and identify ways to improve, plus attend to special administrative measures, including, where appropriate, the payment of agreed fees. It is also the final opportunity to clarify intellectual property rights and ongoing communications and address minor issues. Finally, it is also a segue to secure new or ongoing work.

Closure begins with an agreement that the assignment has been completed, usually following the agreed service provision and meeting the consulting contract's terms. However, early termination may sometimes occur by revising the initial agreement. The outcomes of the closure stage should be to release all parties from their contracted obligations and ensure a common understanding of continuing commitments, such as confidentiality, data protection, intellectual property rights, and guarantees. It is also time to finalise the payment of fees and expenses.

Legal and Contractual Matters

The consultant is responsible for ensuring adequate processes are in place to ensure all aspects of the consulting agreement have been dealt with expeditiously. This process includes reconciling all expense claims, issuing invoices, and finalising outstanding payments. In addition, it involves releasing all resources, including any sub-contractors, providing warranties and guarantees, protecting third-party confidentiality, intellectual property and other rights, and ensuring formal sign-off and acceptance of the project's completion.

Administrative and Communication Matters

As it is for managing an assignment's legal and contractual matters, so it is that the consultant must be sure to have effective and efficient administrative and document control processes in place. These procedures include ensuring that all administrative issues are concluded efficiently. They also require that data is protected and backed up; confidentiality agreements are in place; client property, equipment, and facilities are returned in good order; sub-contractors, if any, are released or recruited; all internal quality assurance procedures have been fulfilled; and communication obligations are satisfied. In addition, government projects might require compliance with document security aspects such as the length of storage and the protection of project files.

Assignment and Performance Evaluation and Improvement

Perhaps the most valuable outcome of a project is the opportunity to evaluate your and your team's performance, assess the effectiveness of your work, and explore new ways to improve. An objective observer best considers using metrics specified by the client and consulting team in consultation. Post-assignment evaluation might also be a contractual condition.

Timing is essential to a practical evaluation. From experience, two evaluation periods are needed. The first should be undertaken as soon as practicable following project closure. The second, sometime later, is to assess whether or not recommendations have been or are being implemented and the effectiveness of outcomes. The scheduling of the second evaluation will depend on the assignment's nature and advice and should be agreed upon in consultation with stakeholders. It is an excellent chance to identify any need for further intervention and skills transfer.

The nature and extent of an assignment will determine the metrics to be evaluated. However, specific topics for evaluation include client satisfaction, training needs, communication effectiveness, team performance, process and innovation effectiveness and improvements, and stakeholder benefits. It is also an excellent opportunity to secure referred leads for a new consulting business.

So far, you have learnt something about the management consulting profession and its structure, what a consultant does, the expectations of clients, and the consulting process. The following chapters introduce the process of becoming a professional management consultant, ethical practices that must be followed, client and project identification, and professional development opportunities and requirements. Lastly, there is an exploration of the future for consulting in a volatile, uncertain, complex, and ambiguous world.

Note

1 For example, see SA/SNZ HB 168:2017 "Document Control" at Store | Standards Australia.

7 Creating a Professional Consulting Business

> Success in management requires learning as fast as the world is changing.
>
> (Warren Bennis, 1925–2014)

Starting on the Big Adventure

Are you thinking of setting up your practice? Starting a business can be cheap, quickly undertaken, and trouble-free, like entering a marriage. But, also like a marriage, once begun, it is then that the hard work starts. Business structures vary from country to country and sometimes state to state, but the questions and principles in most jurisdictions are much the same (Table 6). If you work alone, you can begin as a sole trader or proprietor. Then, all that may be needed is to hang up your shingle and start work. However, your business might still need to be registered in some places. For example, in Australia, you must acquire an Australian Business Number (ABN) from the Australian Business Register if you enter a partnership, issue invoices, or claim back tax incurred on operational purchases [60].

However, a partnership or company structure might be more appropriate if you are working as one of two or more practitioners. The most critical first step is to find and engage an accountant you trust to advise you. Everyone's circumstances are different, and the tax and other legal commitments in each geographic area necessitate you taking advice on the best structure(s) to protect yourself and your family and optimise tax obligations. You should also seek legal support to create applicable agreements between you and others involved in the business and a trust deed to protect your family's assets. While accounting and legal costs can mount quickly, ensuring that you get the suitable structures and agreements in place from the outset will be well worth the investment in the long term.

Different jurisdictions have variations on the above. Therefore, seeking legal and accounting advice before deciding which structure best suits your business

DOI: 10.4324/9781003466987-7

Table 6 Common business structures – their upsides and downsides

Structure	Reason	Upsides	Downsides
Sole trader (proprietorship)	For a solo operator.	It has a low set-up cost and is simple to create. Low tax obligations, but A separate bank account is not needed, but You are the sole owner and responsible for all business decisions. There are relatively few administration and reporting requirements.	You are responsible for all debts and losses of the business. Personal income tax rates apply to income generated. While a separate bank account is unnecessary, separating business and personal expenses is recommended. You can be sued for breach of contract as an individual.
Trust	In this case, a trustee is responsible for the business's operations.	The Trustee owns the business and is responsible for all business decisions, losses, and debts. The Trustee has discretion on who benefits from the trust. It provides some asset protection and tax advantages.	It is complex to set up. The establishment and exit costs can be high. Tax obligations can be high. Moderate legal obligations. A separate bank account is required. There are added administration and reporting requirements.
Partnership	A typical structure for professionals. It allows two or more people to distribute income or losses from the business.	It can be as simple as a handshake, agreeing to be partners, but Low tax obligations. You and your partners own the business and are responsible for all business decisions. There are low to medium legal obligations.	Each partner may be jointly and severally liable for debts incurred by the others, so partnership agreements are strongly recommended. As a result, set-up costs can be moderate to high. A separate bank account is required. There are added administrative and reporting costs.
Company	A company is a person in its own right. It can limit the liability of its owners to some extent, enter into contracts, and be sued.	A company is owned by its shareholders and managed by the directors (who may or may not hold shares. The directors are responsible for all business decisions. In jurisdictions influenced by British Law, the presence of a "corporate veil" means that the company, not individual directors, is usually, but not always, responsible for the debts and losses of the company. Depending on company income, there may be some tax advantages.	Set-up costs can be high. Legal and accounting costs can also be high. Moderate tax obligations. Breaches of the director's statutory duties can result in heavy penalties, including prison. In some cases, directors may incur personal liability for debts incurred by the business and may be sued for negligence.

and personal needs is wise. While you can change the business structure later, to do that can be pretty costly. So, getting it right the first time is the best policy.

Business Planning

It is an often-stated cliché that businesses that fail to plan, plan to fail. Having a clear business plan is essential for success. Proper planning means proper investigation. Take time to conduct the research needed, as you would for your clients. Get to understand the industry via a 5-Forces analysis and, especially, do a thorough PESTEL analysis to fully understand the environment(s) you are entering. If international consulting is envisaged, do that for each country and combine it with a national risk assessment. Spend time in each market you are planning to enter.

Desktop research is acceptable for a broad understanding of a market, but nothing replaces on-ground study. Speak with potential clients to get a comprehensive understanding of their needs. Learn about local regulatory constraints. Do you need a special licence before you can practice? Will you need a special visa? Are there language barriers? What are the cultural norms and mores? What are the technical barriers? For example, while many electronic devices can be used internationally, not all can. Power supplies, plug types, and electrical safety requirements vary from country to country. Access to familiar websites might be blocked, so what options are available? How will you get around? Find out about public transport options, how to access them, and how to avoid the traps.[1] What are the business and living costs associated with operating in a different region or country? Finally, what are the safety and security concerns, and how can those be mitigated?

When you have completed your research, start documenting your plan. First, what is the purpose of your business to be? Where do you want it to be in one, three, five, and ten years? Next, complete a SWOT analysis of your practice for each market. Who are your competitors? What are their strengths and weaknesses? Why will clients choose your business over your competitors? How will your potential clients know about you and your offerings?

A core activity of any professional consultancy is document management and security. How will you control your internal documents? How will you ensure the safety of those of your clients? How will you control document access? How will you ensure that malware and computer viruses don't contaminate your systems? How will you back up data to be safe and restored in case of system failure or blockage? To guide you when developing document control processes, adhere to international standards, such as ISO 9001 and ISO 27001.

The key to your plan will be showing investors and lenders how you can fund your business's operations over time. That means having a detailed and realistic understanding of expenses and potential revenue. One rule of thumb: when you have completed your budget, double the expenses and halve the revenue projections. If the budget still shows that you will be profitable, or at least cashflow positive, go ahead. If not, reconsider. Ask trusted others to run a reality check on your assumptions and numbers, and don't be offended if they tell you your plan is unrealistic. They may be doing you an enormous favour.

Planning well will save you time and money later and may be the difference between success and failure.

Pricing Your Consulting Services

The price you can get for your consulting services will depend on four factors: the cost of running your practice, your expectations of financial return, the uniqueness of your services, and what the market is prepared to pay for those. But, of course, that assumes that you have a fix on your costs, your expectations are realistic, and that you know current pricing levels for services that are equivalent to yours.

To understand profitability in a consulting practice, Maister [27, 61] developed a variant of the DuPont model referred to earlier, replacing "return on equity" with "profit per partner", as seen in the following formula:

$$\underset{\text{(Profitability)}}{\frac{\text{Profits}}{\text{Partners}}} = \underset{\text{(Margin)}}{\frac{\text{Profits}}{\text{Fees}}} \times \underset{\text{(Productivity)}}{\frac{\text{Fees}}{\text{Consultants}}} \times \underset{\text{(Leverage)}}{\frac{\text{Consultants}}{\text{Partners}}}$$

Maister's model is commonly used in firms with multiple partners and consultants and is appropriate for them. However, most consultancies consist of just one consultant. For the sole operator, profitability is determined by your operating costs, expectations of financial return, your services' uniqueness, and your clients' propensity to pay for those. Knowing your overall costs then is fundamental to your ability to set a price for your advice. So, a simple pricing model is as follows:

Total business costs = variable + fixed + depreciation and amortisation + interest (TBCy) per year/working days per year (TBCd)/7.5 working hours per day = Total business costs per hour (TBCh).

As a baseline, double your TBCh to determine an hourly billing rate. That rate may then need to be adjusted to meet market expectations of the value provided by your services.

There are more complex pricing models, so you should seek advice from your accountant on whether or not a different model will better suit your practice.

Promoting Your Business

For all markets, to be successful as a management consultant, you must be of value to your clients. They will seek a person or organisation with integrity and technical competence. The ILO has proposed seven principles for marketing consulting. Number one is the obligation to "regard the client's needs and requirements as the focal point of all marketing" [27, p. 649]. Table 7 lists and explains the ILO's principles.

If you have any previous clients, ask them what benefits they got from your advice. What is your value proposition?

A value proposition is a short, convincing statement that tells customers what tangible and intangible benefits they will earn from buying a service from your practice [62, 63]. It also explains how your offering differs or is better than your competitors. The value you are offering clients must be clearly stated. Write it down, limit it to one or two sentences, and rehearse until it flows naturally from your tongue. It will form the basis of your promotional activity. Make your value statement a prominent part of your website and highlight it on all promotional material.

How consultancies promote their services is under increasing scrutiny, particularly for publicly funded projects. The increase in oversight follows

Table 7 The ILO's seven fundamental principles for marketing consulting [27]

ILO's fundamental principles	Comment
Regard the clients' needs and requirements as the focal point of all marketing.	Clients are looking for your advice and assistance. While they might be happy to hear that you are brilliant and successful, that doesn't necessarily help them. They need assurance that you understand their organisation, the challenges they face, and that you have or can create solutions and muster the resources that will help them.
Remember that every client is unique.	Beware of overly relying on your experience and case studies to help you; it can be a trap. Remember that each organisation comprises different people with different values, skills and attributes and is unique. The challenges they face must be viewed in that light.
Don't misrepresent yourself.	This principle is pure and simply an ethical issue. A self-inflated level of confidence in your abilities might tempt you to take on work for which you are unqualified. To do so is unethical.
Don't oversell.	Overpromising and underdelivering will likely end up in tears and may be unethical.
Refrain from denigrating other consultants.	Be factual in any response. Clients will view you as unprofessional if you give biased opinions. Stick to the facts, or avoid commenting altogether.
Never forget that you are marketing a professional service.	Clients might be looking to you to provide innovative solutions to their challenges. While you may need to be entrepreneurial and forceful when promoting your services, remember you are a professional advisor, not a snake oil salesperson.
Aim at an equally high professional performance in marketing and execution.	Ensuring the best outcomes for your clients is the finest possible marketing. Clients will refer you and bring you back for new projects. Of course, the opposite is true if your performance and outcomes are suboptimal.

several reported cases of conflict of interest between a firm's consulting and financial functions and a practice of building in future work for consultants from one project to another [64, 65]. Some have labelled this latter practice as a type of insider trading and called for greater centralised control of government consulting projects [66]. However, you can avoid falling into a conflict trap by following your values and the sound ethical principles in the IMC's Code of Conduct.

There are many ways to promote your business and raise market awareness of the value offered by your practice. An excellent first step is joining a professional industry network like IMC Australia. The benefits are four-fold. First, membership provides an environment for continual learning and development, potentially culminating in an internationally recognised CMC qualification. Second, it facilitates access to other professional management consultants worldwide with varied types of experience and areas of specialisation. It thereby provides opportunities to form multi-disciplinary project teams. Third, by joining, you demonstrate to your clients that you are a trusted, ethical professional group member. Lastly, membership enables access to various discounted products, such as professional insurance and research support.

The Importance of Trust

As a consultant, trust will be the cornerstone of your practice, not just for capital raising but for securing and sustaining ongoing work. Reputation building is the foundation for building a successful management consulting practice. It's a bit like a pinball game: you win one game, and then you get to play another. As you undertake successful projects, your reputation will grow. Don't be afraid to ask your clients for referrals. Join networks where your potential clients gather. Perhaps previous or current clients will be willing to introduce you to their peers. However, always respect client confidentiality, even if that means missing out on future work. Remember, your reputation is your greatest asset and must be protected. After years of building, trust and reputation can be destroyed by just one thoughtless act or word, and at that point, your career is finished.

Managing Your Business Growth

The rate at which you choose to grow your practice will depend on several critical factors:

1   Your life goals
2   The level of family support you have for the venture
3   Who and where is your market located

4   Your ability to access the capital you need to enable your growth plan to be successful
5   Your willingness and ability to control costs
6   Your physical and mental capacity to manage growth
7   PESTEL constraints

Businesses don't fail just because they make a loss; they fail because they have run out of money or no longer have access to it. So, it is not unusual for a business to be a lossmaker for a year or two or longer and become very successful. However, such a scenario demands that you have access to secure lines of capital from trusted sources and keep business costs as low as possible for as long as possible.

Getting Access to the Funds You Need

Early access to funds often comes from one or more of four sources: the owner's savings, their friends, their family, and borrowings. Seek legal advice before approaching others. There can be heavy fines or even jail time awaiting those who attempt to attract investment from the general public without putting the protections required by law in place. Investors must trust the owner(s) and have confidence that their business model is sound, a reasonable financial return is likely, and the organisation's values align with theirs. Having a credible business plan will help give comfort to potential funders.

Controlling Cash Flow

Always know how much cash you have available for your business. Revenue generation and cost control must be the primary foci for business owners. If you are a solo operator, and internet access and speed are sufficient and reliable, work from a place like your home or garage, where rent costs are not an added burden. Keep property costs as low as possible for as long as possible. Then, when it comes time to move into an external office, look to buy a suitable place and allow for growth. The property will be an asset of the business that can be leveraged to fund future expansion or sold as part of an exit strategy.

Closely track your business expenses and accounts receivable. Securing progress payments from the beginning of a project will help. Therefore, a precise payment plan must be a core element of client proposals.

Having an Exit Strategy

Not all businesses succeed. Most don't. A strategic choice may be that you must exit the business to protect your reputation and your family's assets.

Winding up a business can be tricky – emotionally and financially. However, it might be the best solution for all concerned. Available options include:

1   Sell all or part of the practice as an ongoing concern. To achieve this, the business must be of value to the buyer. If the firm relies on one of two people, it has no value when they leave. Typically, having secure ongoing contracts that don't rely on your presence, loyal and regular clients, proveable client acceptance of the expected outcome, fixed assets of value, protected technological, procedural, or other intellectual property, and a strong brand reputation will help.
2   Facilitate a merger of your practice with another with a similar business model, values, and access to capital. While also a growth option, a union may allow you to exit the business gracefully with your reputation intact and be financially beneficial.
3   Controlled closure. Make sure to consult your accounting and legal advisers before you start. A controlled closure will involve complex steps, including staff retrenchment, liquidating assets, terminating leases and client contracts, finalising supply and support agreements, and deregistering the business. If done well, your reputation will be retained and court time avoided.

Your exit strategy should avoid a forced liquidation that will damage your reputation, result in high legal costs, and may land you in court for years following the venture's end.

You now have a business with all of the potential that it brings. It's time to embed the ethics required to make it a growing and sustainable entity.

Note

1 Taxi drivers are notorious in some places for charging what they think you can pay, which is likely many times the regular fare. Also beware of airport intercepts by willing drivers.

8 Ethical Practice as the Basis of Good Decision-Making

> Love all, trust a few, do wrong to none.
>
> (William Shakespeare, 1564–1616)

Ethics is a system of moral principles that guide us on how to live a good life, our rights and responsibilities, our language, and our decisions about good and evil. Ethics defines what is good for individuals and society. The word is derived from *ethos*, meaning custom, habit, character, or disposition. Our ethics define us. It is who we are, what we do, and where we live [67].

A key characteristic of professional practice includes a set of recognised ethical norms shared and applied by the profession's members. In addition, an agreed code of conduct should be observed to guide each consultant's ethical and professional conduct during an assignment. This code of conduct includes professional behaviour, sustainability, social responsibility, conflict of interest, and integrity [40].

In Australia, the standards for CMCs and those who work with them can be found in the IMC Australia *Code of Professional Conduct and Ethics* ("the Code")(Appendix D). Together with the interpretation statements, the code clearly defines what is proper in conducting business as a professional management consultant. In addition, code development guidelines have been laid down in ISO20700:2017 [40]. The code applies to all IMC members, who must sign a declaration of adherence when they apply for membership. However, CMCs are held to a higher standard, and for them, an ethical breach may invoke the activation of disciplinary procedures.

Many professional organisations, such as those representing management consultants, lawyers, architects, and engineers, have developed their codes of ethics, and these codes help the members put ethics into practice. For example, in management consulting, ethics can best be defined as the voluntary assumption of an obligation to exercise judgement and self-discipline above and beyond legal requirements. However, the norms in the code demand more

DOI: 10.4324/9781003466987-8

Table 8 Examples of guidelines for management consultancy service providers (MCSP) for a code of conduct [Institute of Management Consultants (Australia) cited in 40, p. 22]

Ethical principle	Manifestation of principle
Responsibility to the public	
Efficiency	Optimising personal, client, and other resources to complete an assignment.
Sustainability	Recommending solutions compatible with sustainable development principles and aligned with the United Nations Sustainability Goals10F10F.[a]
Responsibility	Representing the interests of the consultancy industry to the broader community.
Legal	Being aware of and complying with applicable laws and regulations relevant to the assignment.
	Not causing anyone to contravene any applicable laws and regulations during the assignment.
Public confidence	By conducting their activities at all times in a manner that fosters confidence in the profession.
Responsibility to the profession	
Respect for the profession	Exhibiting conduct that reflects honourably upon and enhances the standing and public regard of the profession.
Integrity and professionalism	Respect the rights of other professionals in the consultancy industry by not using proprietary information or methodolosgies without permission.
	Maintaining disciplinary mechanisms to uphold the code of conduct.

[a]The 17 goals | sustainable development (un.org).

than respecting the law. After all, perfectly legal behaviour may not always be considered entirely ethical, and as we all know, the law can sometimes be an ass.

In many situations, though, it is not always possible to refer to the letter of the code or a formal declaration of norms by an employer to know genuine professional and ethical behaviour. Therefore, management consultants must be guided by their ethics and conduct based on their background, development, beliefs, and perception of what is proper or improper and beneficial or not to the community, the client, and other stakeholders. It is incumbent on those in professional practice to hone their ethical barometer through training, research, and diligence. Table 8 lists conduct guidelines for management consultancy service providers (MCSP).

Several moral theories have evolved over the centuries and are relevant to applying ethics in management consulting. While no one is universally superior to others, it is startling how they agree when applied to common ethical problems. As a result, they are well worth studying by any professional.

Ethical Theories

There are two primary schools in moral philosophy: consequentialism and deontology. The four theories shown in Table 9 are examples of each. In consequential ethics, all action aims to achieve the greatest happiness for the most significant number of people. Subscribers to the consequential school of thought, for example, Aristotle and Mills, hold that ethical decisions are based on outcomes. In other words, the consequences of a person's conduct are the ultimate basis for determining right from wrong. However, in deontology (non-consequential) ethics, those who subscribe to this school, for instance, Kant and Locke, believe that people base their decisions on rational and deeply held values of duty and obligation to others.

Consequentialism may be fraught. For example, if it is in the majority's best interests for one to be killed, then that would be an ethical outcome for the consequentialist, notwithstanding that the dead individual may have been innocent. Unfortunately, it is sometimes challenging to balance the two ethical schools. We have seen that dilemma play out in the recent COVID-19

Table 9 Consequential v non-consequential ethics

Consequentialism	Deontology, or non-consequential
Aristotle's Virtue-based Ethics	*Kant's Duty-based ethics*
Aristotle argued that happiness is achieved by developing virtues or character qualities through deduction and reason. An act is good if it is reasonable. Reasonableness usually means a course of action that is the golden mean between extremes of excess and deficiency. Conflict can occur when the definition of "virtue" is occasionally vague and challenging in specific cases. However, seeking an ideal point between two extremes is frequently helpful in ethics.	Kant maintained that everyone must follow the courses of action that would be acceptable or universal principles for everyone to follow Kant's "universal law" is to be found in the writings of all major religions. For example, "And as you wish that others would do to you, do so to them" (Luke 6:31). Conflicts that arise following a universal principle may cause harm For example, telling a 'white' lie is unacceptable, even if the truth causes damage.
Mills Utilitarianism	*Locke's Rights-based Ethics*
Mill proposed that an action is morally correct if it produces the most significant benefit for most people. In addition, the duration, intensity, and equality of distribution of the advantages should be considered. When evaluating the benefits, a conflict of interest may arise. This possibility arises because personal use must be counted as equal to a similar advantage to another.	Locke asserted that all persons are free and equal, and each has a right to life, health, liberty, possessions, and the product of their labour. Conflict might arise as it is sometimes difficult to determine when one person's rights infringe on those of another.

pandemic. In that case, the pressure to protect as many as possible from disease conflicted with the damage caused to the economy.

Professional Conduct

Management consultants in many countries have established voluntary professional associations to represent their common interests. These associations play a leading role in promoting professional management consulting standards, gaining management's confidence, and promoting the reputation of management consultants in society. Perhaps most importantly, these organisations guide consultants' ethical practices and enforce codes of professional conduct.

The code identifies those obligations that protect the public and the client. It also recognises members' expectations concerning other participants and the profession.

The following summarises the content of the code in force in Australia. The Australian Code is like codes for other national professional management consulting organisations. In addition, it now forms the basis for a Universal Code of Conduct promoted by CMC-Global. Therefore, the complete code and its *Statements of Interpretation* are integral to this guide for CMCs in Australia.

1. Management consultants must maintain the dignity and prestige of the profession. They must not damage it in any way.
2. Management consultants must consider their responsibilities to the public and the profession. Therefore, they must act according to the law and may not speak on behalf of the profession without appropriate authorisation.
3. Management consultants must act in their client's best interests, providing professional services with integrity, objectivity, and independence. Other responsibilities to the client are strictures regarding competency and ensuring clients are fully informed regarding how an assignment will be carried out and for what fee. Conflicts of interest must be declared. Client confidentiality must be maintained.
4. Management consultants are responsible for other members in that they must inform another member before critically reviewing that member's work. In addition, a consultant must report the unbecoming professional conduct of another member.
5. Members are also expected to be conversant with the profession's Common Body of Knowledge and keep abreast of developments in any job area where specific expertise is claimed.
6. Anyone working under the leadership or direction of a member must act within the bounds of the code.

These obligations require that individual practitioners maintain familiarity with the code.

The Cost of Practice Malfeasance

The consequences of breaches of ethical behaviour by professional management consultants are fourfold. First, they affect the individual consultants, potentially ending their careers and resulting in criminal charges and lawsuits. Second, they affect the client, whose trust and business have been compromised. Third, they damage the reputation of the consultant's company and might lead to financial ruin. Finally, they damage the profession's standing as a whole, leading to a loss of public confidence in management consultants in general.

The Disciplinary Approach Used in Australia

Members of the IMC in Australia are required to comply with the following prescribed standards, which contain the disciplinary procedures to be followed when a complaint is made about other members, a member by the public, or a client:

1   Code of Professional Conduct and Ethics
2   Articles of Association, Memorandum of Association and By-laws of the Institute of Management Consultants, Australia

Where the Disciplinary Committee and the Federal Council of the Institute agree, a member who behaves in a manner detrimental to the profession may be suspended or expelled from membership or have other penalties applied to them.

Those affected are encouraged to contact the Institute for specifics on this disciplinary process.

Application of the Code in Consulting Assignments

A member of the IMC in Australia is responsible to several stakeholders to prevent acts or omissions that harm or could cause damage to the public, other consulting members of IMC Australia or clients. They must make themselves aware of those aspects of their work or public activities that could breach professional conduct and plan the steps required to avoid a breach and manage any risk of harm. For example, when leading a team on a project, the member must ensure that everyone under their direction adheres to the code – Table 10 lists familiar sources of conflict of interest.

Issues That May Arise during the Consulting Process

The code's "responsibility to the client" section has been created to guard against unethical or unprofessional conduct. From contracting to closure, every step in the consulting process requires a professional consultant to conduct due diligence and be aware of the code's applicability.

Table 10 Potential sources of a conflict of interest [IMC (Australia), cited by 40, p. 23]

Source	Explanation
Multiple projects with the same client at a different level or different location	Are there parallel or similar contracts in the same group, past or present?
The client is a former client.	Where a client is also a former client, has the MCSP provided previous advice or conducted an earlier analysis that would constrain the MCSP's direction in the new situation?
MCSP has a client or a former client in the same industry	Where the MCSP has a current or former client, perhaps in the same industry as the client that the MCSP now seeks to advise, does the MCSP have proprietary information that could impact its advice?
Staff members have a relationship.	Do any staff members at the MCSP have family relationships with client staff members, particularly those in management positions?
Internal consulting organisations	Do any staff members at the MCSP have hierarchical relationships with client or recipient staff members, particularly those in management positions?
MCSP or staff have a financial interest	Does the MCSP or its staff members have a financial interest in the client or its management team members, including an overdue account receivable, loan or equity investment?
MCSP has an audit relationship	Where the MCSP also has a financial audit relationship with the client, are the prospective consulting services allowed by the relevant securities regulator? Note that where a client is also an audit client but not subject to securities regulation, the client's audit committee may choose to restrict the additional services of the MCSP as a matter of policy.
Other	Other business relationships may include situations where the MCSP or its staff have a shared interest with a client in a third-party contract (such as a software partnership, leased premises, a subscription to sports tickets, etc.) or where the MCSP or its staff members are "captive" on the staff of the client, as in the case of "contract" or "interim" management or "internal consultants".

First Contact

Concerning the first contact with a potential client, the consultant must sincerely present their scope, work plan and costs, level of competence, and experience. The client must also be fully informed of the assignment objectives in writing.

Diagnostic Phase

During diagnosis, present the findings fully and as accurately as possible and make recommendations in your client's best interest (the code defines the client as "the organisation"). Note that those interests must not conflict with your ethical and societal responsibilities.

Ongoing

Once an assignment has begun, the consultant must concentrate on the client's and the public's needs and, through openness, transparency, and ongoing dialogue, avoid abusing client and employee trust. For example, a member must keep confidential any information obtained during an assignment unless permission is given, preferably in writing, to share that knowledge. Confidentiality includes not identifying the client's name or employees who have provided critical intelligence.

Potential remedies include the following:

- *Seek consent*: In certain circumstances, you may be able to manage conflicts through full disclosure of past or current client relationships, seeking the written approval/consent of the affected parties.
- *Isolate areas of potential conflict of interest*: Establish confidentiality/non-disclosure agreements concerning new client information, staffing restrictions, separation of service teams and data, differing client reporting points, and other approaches.
- *Termination*: You may be unable to manage or mitigate a conflict and will be required to turn down an assignment.

Questions to Ask When Faced with an Ethical Dilemma

There will be times in your career when you are faced with an ethical dilemma, the answer to which is not apparent to you. When that happens, answering the following questions may provide a helpful guide [41]:

1 Have I reflected on or consulted with the Code Administrator about whether I am compromising my responsibilities under the code?
2 Have I considered the issue from a legal perspective?
3 Have I investigated whether my behaviour aligns with a policy or procedure of my IMC or CMC-Global?
4 Could my private interests or relationships be viewed as impairing my objectivity?
5 Could my decision or action be viewed as resulting in personal gain, financial or otherwise?
6 Could my decision or action be viewed as furthering the private interests of someone with whom I have a significant personal or business relationship?
7 Could my decisions or actions be perceived as granting or receiving preferential treatment?

8 Have I disclosed all conflicts of interest to my client(s)?

9 Am I proud of my decision or actions?

10 Given that they know the circumstances, would my family be proud of my decision or actions?

If you must answer no to any of those questions, reconsider your course of action. If you don't care about the answers, choose another vocation.

To this point, you have read about the profession, the requirements for professionalism, the expectations of clients, your role as a professional management consultant, and the ethical expectations of those institutes and world governing bodies overseeing the consulting profession. Now, it's time to give thought to your ongoing development and learning.

9   Professional Development

> A person going nowhere can be sure of reaching his destination. Take the first step in faith. You don't have to see the whole staircase – just take the first step.
>
> (Martin Luther King Jr., 1929–1968)

Maintaining Thought Leadership

Professional management consultants are often viewed as thought leaders and innovators by their clients. To sustain that esteemed position, consultants must continually update their knowledge and skills to maintain relevance and ensure their advice is the best possible. This expectation means gaining experience and making sure that your qualifications are still relevant and your professional certifications are current. Take part regularly in specialist updates run by your university or college. Take courses in topics of interest, and upgrade your formal qualifications whenever you feel it is needed to keep your knowledge current and leading edge. Above all, continue to hone your critical thinking skills.

Learn to Live and Work with Ambiguity

As I've already discussed, consultants frequently have to work in an ambiguous environment with no right or wrong answers, just outcomes that are either favourable or unfavourable. Finding the most fitting and least damaging solution becomes the challenge. Sharpening your analysis and decision-making skills is crucial for success in such an environment.

Cherish Your Baseline Education

No matter your level of qualification, your baseline education will continue to provide direction and assist you in your consulting career. Modern school and

DOI: 10.4324/9781003466987-9

tertiary education programs are designed to guide students in critical thinking and research that will guide them to find information and use models that have been tried and tested to work in most circumstances. We all tend to forget about the models we learned in business school. They are seen as an old hack, or memorising them was just a part of passing a course. But, you might be surprised to discover that many work in real-life situations. After all, in the main, they were based on sound research. Basic mathematics, writing, speaking and non-verbal communication skills, analytical methods, relationship building, reading, computer operation skills, and curiosity were all formed or enhanced during your time in pre-professional education. Cherish and continue to develop that learning.

Gain Experience

Experience is the best but sometimes the most demanding and cruel teacher. However, experience is the only way to develop and hone your professional skills and understand your work's situational realities. Working with clients one-on-one will be a significant learning experience if you are alone. Have faith in your knowledge and abilities. If you are part of a team of consultants, rely on and learn from each team member. Ideally, they will have had more experience in the areas where you are unsure and perhaps more knowledge. Be a sponge and absorb everything around you. You are never too young, too old, or too experienced that you cannot learn from each event. Occasionally, you might slip and fall. Get back up, learn from all that went wrong, and move on. The next time, you will be much better placed to give sound advice due to that slip. You will need at least three to five years of experience as a professional management consultant to gain CMC status.

Learn Continuously

Continually upgrade and modernise your knowledge. While no one is omniscient, the more you know, the more robust will be the advice you can give. Participate in professional development activities, often free to IMC members or other professional bodies, and in network groups, such as your alumni association. Your IMC and CMC-Global run frequent interactive professional development programs via Linkedin, Zoom, Teams, and YouTube to help you stay current with events and industry trends. Newsletters and journal publications are also valuable sources of contemporary thinking by experts in their fields. Discussion meetings with other IMC members enable a free-flowing exchange of ideas on challenges faced and new approaches. In addition, contributions by the pool of CMC-Global Academic Fellows provide access to current and evolving research.

Set aside time each week for study. It doesn't have to be much; just an hour or two a week will support your quest to remain at the top of your game. Learn something new every day. Whether what you have learnt is seen as significant at the time or not, in the end, it all adds to the total of your knowledge and experience and will help develop your decision-making ability.

Hone Your Communication Skills

No matter how brilliant your ideas and solutions are, they will not be accepted if you cannot communicate them clearly to your colleagues and clients. Learn and practise your communication skills and strive to be the best communicator you know. Your advice will not be considered credible unless you can communicate it clearly and concisely, verbally and in writing. So, constantly improving your communication skills must become a lifetime endeavour.

As your career develops, public speaking will become essential to your armoury. Avoid making PowerPoint your messenger. It is a tool to support your presentation, not vice versa. Join an organisation like Toastmasters that will allow you to learn and practise the craft of public speaking in a non-threatening environment – as with writing, perfecting your speaking in front of small and large audiences must be a constant pursuit.

Recognise and Address Knowledge Gaps

For the professional management consultant, understanding your knowledge limitations is essential. None of us knows it all (I used to, but I've forgotten a lot). So it would help if you worked hard to fill in the gaps in your knowledge, especially in those areas crucial to your profession. Conduct a self-SWOT analysis. Take courses; read journal articles, books, and research reports; attend seminars and workshops; attend networking events, and discuss topics of concern with your peers. However you do it, you must identify the gaps in your knowledge and then work hard to fill them with credible and relevant facts. Now, as I've stated already, none of us is omniscient. So, for gaps beyond filling or of no interest, attach yourself to someone with the necessary knowledge. As with a firm, the broader the knowledge base you can give to an assignment, the more innovative and credible your solutions will be.

Earn Professional Certification

With certification comes credibility. Larger consulting firms often have their accreditation models and established brands. However, most professional management consultants don't work for large firms; they are single or small team operators. Even those who work for big consulting groups are very likely to work as individuals on a project, albeit supported by a more substantial team and infrastructure. The preeminent professional certification for all individual management consultants is the "CMC" (Certified Management Consultant). The CMC is an internationally recognised qualification issued by IMCs worldwide and CMC-Global through the CMC-Global Institute. Certification provides clients with certainty that the holder is serious about their consulting career and has the knowledge, processes, ethics, and commitment to assist them appropriately. Qualification is peer-reviewed, rigorous, and based on an applicant's knowledge, skills, competence, and integrity. Assessors will consider your consulting experience, competency, understanding of the Consulting Process, acceptance of and adherence to the Uniform Code of Professional Conduct, and academic qualifications.

However, for most, the road to CMC certification is long, typically three to five years. However, the conceptual professional development pathway developed by CMC-Global, detailed below, allows for intermediate steps that culminate in eventual certification by your IMC.

The Path to Your CMC

As Figure 20 shows, CMC-Global's conceptual pathway consists of four levels:

1   Foundation level – the successful completion of ISO 20700 training and or demonstrated understanding of ISO 20700:2017 Guidelines
2   Mid-level accreditation
3   CMC-Global Registered Consultant level
4   CMC award

Achieving Foundation Level Recognition

The Foundation Level involves you being able to demonstrate your understanding of ISO 20700:2017 Guidelines. Your IMC will likely run courses on this topic and provide a self-declaration checklist to help you. There is also an

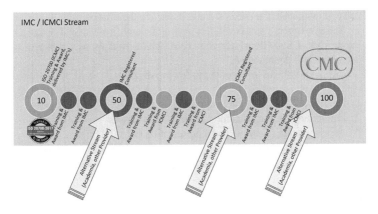

Figure 20 ICMCI professional development path concept from entry level to gold standard ([68] published with permission).

assumption that you have acquired the technical and academic qualifications needed to be a professional advisor.

Achieving Mid-Level Certification

Mid-level certification is achieved by you completing the CMC-Global training program. Program elements can be delivered by any CMC-Global accredited provider, such as your IMC, or as part of an accredited university undergraduate or postgraduate program. They may be offered as a series of micro-credentials or in full-time mode. Completing this level will result in your recognition by CMC-Global as a Registered Consultant.

Achieving CMC-Global Registration

You are almost there! By this stage, you will have achieved sufficient experience to demonstrate superior technical knowledge, professional competence, continual adherence to industry standards and policies, and high ethical standards.

Achieving the Ultimate – Becoming a Certified Management Consultant

The CMC is a competency-based qualification that requires you to demonstrate sufficient, relevant, and timely evidence of your competency as a management consultant. You must be a current professional member of your IMC and show that you understand and adhere to the Code of Ethics and Consultant's Pledge (Appendix B) to be eligible to apply for a CMC.

To achieve certification, you must prove continuous practice as a management consultant during the last three years, demonstrate proficiency against all areas in the Competency Framework, and provide evidence that clients value your contribution, delivery, and impact on their business.

The assessment process will test your proficiency against the Competence Framework. CMC-Global accredits each IMC triennially to assess applications for CMC qualification.

CMC Assessment involves the following steps:

1 Review of your completed application by your IMC
2 Forwarding your application to a panel of assessors
3 An assessment interview and a presentation by you
4 An assessment panel review of all evidence against the Competency Framework to ensure a minimum of two forms of evidence for each competency area
5 Client reference checks
6 Forwarding Assessment Panel recommendations to the CMC Chair
7 If successful, the award of your CMC by a representative of your IMC

The CMC mark, which you can signal by using the "CMC" post-nominal designation, gives your clients the confidence that they have engaged a professional who will deliver the highest level of management consulting. It assures them that you have completed a rigorous certification process and have a record of successful assignments. It also shows that you have been endorsed by recognised practitioners and demonstrates your ongoing commitment to management consulting as a profession and a career. Finally, it shows that you have had a history of continuing professional development and are committed to your profession's Code of Ethics.

Your CMC shows clients you have achieved the highest professional standard in the consulting industry and demonstrates your commitment to ongoing professional development. The award is internationally portable and recognised in more than fifty countries.

You are entitled to feel very proud of your achievements when, finally, you are awarded your CMC certificate by your IMC. You are now a professional. Bells and whistles are all around! But, you must continue to practise and develop, maintain adherence to the Competency Framework, and renew your CMC qualification every three years.

Your Steps to Professional Success

Professional success is never guaranteed. But if you follow the steps described throughout this book and summarised in Figure 21, add a pinch of dumb luck and not-so-common common sense, you will likely become a professional in demand. Remember, adhere to your and the profession's core values, continually improve your competency, develop and protect your reputation, and success will follow.

Well, you are on your way to a bright and promising career as a management consultant. So, what does the future hold? The next chapter discusses the future of consulting in a volatile, uncertain, complex, and uncertain world. You will need all of your skills, patience, perseverance, resilience, and a little luck. But by maintaining your professionalism, you will succeed.

Figure 21 Your steps to professional success.

10 The Future of Consulting in a VUCA World

> Experts ought to be on tap and not on top.
>
> (George Russell, 1867–1935) [69][1]

In the child's game, hide and seek, a common refrain from the seeker is "Coming, ready or not!" In the world of consulting, change is the seeker. The consultant's role is to prepare their client for the changes that will inevitably come, whether or not they are ready.

We live in volatile, uncertain, complex, and ambiguous (VUCA) times. It is a time of permacrisis[2]. But these times are not unprecedented. Unusual, certainly. Rare even. But this time of the pandemic, war, and climate warming is not unique. Epidemics, pandemics, and wars have happened before, and our planet has warmed and cooled. While this pandemic is not even the first in our lifetime, perhaps it is the most profound. Indeed, it seems so to us. What is different with global warming is that it threatens the human species this time, as do the technologies available to those seeking war. Only through changes to human behaviours can humanity make the changes needed to reverse global warming, mitigate war risks, and save itself.

Although infectious diseases have existed for all humankind, it wasn't until the beginnings of communal living with the agricultural revolution that epidemics and pandemics became more likely. The first recorded was in 430 BC in Athens when an estimated two-thirds of the city's population died, thought to be from typhoid fever. Since then, there have been many.[3] Ravages such as smallpox, the bubonic plague, leprosy, cholera, malaria, measles, influenza, diphtheria, poliomyelitis, and HIV/AIDS are just some. Many others, such as ebola, have threatened. COVID-19 was only the most recent. There will be others.

The rapid worldwide spread of COVID-19 since its first appearance in Wuhan, China, late in 2019 created much uncertainty. Economies were locked down, workforces were decimated in some areas, and global supply chains

DOI: 10.4324/9781003466987-10

were shattered. Healthcare systems were put to the test, and many failed that test. Fearful customers either became reluctant to buy or radically changed their buying habits. Those governments that could afford to have poured billions of dollars into their economies to prevent economic disintegration and the collapse of social cohesion. For those that could not, many more of their citizens died.

According to McKinsey & Company [70], governments will soon face a US$30 trillion fiscal gap. National risk profiles have changed dramatically. Some economies and industry sectors will never recover. Millions of people have died, and millions may still perish before their time because of the virus, the effects of climate change, and war. And yet, not all are suffering. The gap between the 'haves' and 'have nots' continues to grow exponentially.

Consequently, social pressures are building. The Doomsday Clock stands at 90 seconds to midnight. "It is the most dangerous situation humanity has ever faced" [71].

The world's temperatures are rising too quickly. In 2016, Stephen Hawking told BBC News [72] that by 2600, Earth could "become like Venus, with a temperature of 250C and raining sulphuric acid." He later added that humans would need to find another habitable planet within one hundred years if the species is to survive [73]. Governments, industries, and individuals are now concentrating on developing potential mitigants to climate change. Power sources are shifting from fossil fuels to renewables. Motor vehicles are changing from petrol and diesel fuels to battery-run or hydrogen-powered. New ways to control or eliminate contributors to global warming are being developed, and billions of dollars are being spent on the research needed to find hard-found solutions to slow global warming. A revitalised space race has also begun, with entrepreneurs such as Elon Musk, Jeff Bezos, and Richard Branson, plus China, the United States, India, and the European Union all vying to be the first to habitate, and perhaps claim, new worlds to preserve humanity from the perils forecast by Hawking, and access newfound mineral wealth.

So, what does all this mean for consultants and the future? Consultants are in the business of providing independent and unfettered advice. A crucial role is understanding and working out how to deal with uncertainty. They must take the initiative to adapt. To achieve that, the consultant needs to simplify complexity to enhance learning. It also requires the consultant to think strategically; that is, to be fully aware of the futurity of their advice. Sometimes, this comes with developing new technical solutions; at other times, it comes from creating innovative management systems. At the level of government, it means accommodating the migration of people fleeing in fear of their lives or simply for economic advantage and encouraging the importation and assimilation of new skills to fuel new and emerging industries. Frequently, the advice being sought is how to manage the change that flows from the uncertainties of disruption.

Pandemics are significant disruptors. Climate change is, too, as are wars. Since the beginnings of consulting, arguably with the industrial revolution in the late seventeen hundreds, but since Taylor[4] introduced 'science' to the industry in the early 1900s, the consultant has been asked to assist management in clarifying and guiding business directions. Their role has been through world wars, economic upheavals, and pandemics. In a sense, nothing has changed. However, the increasing reliance on artificial intelligence (AI) and the need to manage and make sense of vast amounts of data is different now compared to Taylor's time. Communications, too, have changed. We can now 'zoom' anywhere at any time. So, for the consultant of the twenty-first century, the tools have changed, but not the fundamentals. Consultants must still identify and create solutions to manage complexity and change effectively, but they must also learn to work in and around a metaverse.

The number of consultants available to proffer advice is countercyclical to the economic climate. When the economy is depressed and unemployment, especially among middle and senior managers, is high, the availability of consultants increases. Conversely, the available number of independent advisers decreases when the economy is doing well. At the time of writing, the world's economies are fragile and vulnerable to severe and sudden downturns, so it seems likely that the marketplace for consultants will become more competitive, at least in the short to medium term, but then the cycle will start again. As always, consultants must adapt.

What opportunities lie ahead for those consultants? Well, there are far too many to list. However, as it is now, there will continue to be two types of consultants and, therefore, two kinds of opportunities. The first type is a specialist who knows a lot about a little. The second type is a generalist who knows a little about a great deal. Honesty, credibility, accuracy, ethicality, and the ability to communicate clearly will remain fundamentals for both types. Overarching will be a clear and well-articulated value proposition, reliance on sound methodologies, and the ability to innovate. The need to manage and make sense of vast data and help clients understand their complex environments to drive change will increase while the time available between changes will decrease. Longevity and a reputation for success will flow from that. The focus will be on mitigating and benefiting from climate change and managing supply chains. Those consultants who can survive in this climate will prosper long-term, whether they know a lot about a little or a little about a lot.

As we progress through the twenty-first century, businesses and professional management consultants will face new challenges. The impacts of big data, automation, and artificial intelligence will begin to dominate and demand that consultants gain new and advanced skills in those areas. Periodic restructuring and transformation of the industry is to be expected. In addition, consultants must prepare themselves to help clients develop financial resilience and future-proof asset strategies to cope with future market shocks. Managers will need guidance to prioritise strategies and create a diverse and innovative culture, and building consultant networks and relationship-building will become more critical than ever. Access by consulting firms to online talent platforms such as that launched recently by IMC Australia, CMC Global, and private talent data sources such as that offered by COMATCH will be central to consulting firms subcontracting talent. Forming and understanding relationships will be essential for a successful professional management consultant in such an environment.

As part of the larger business world, management consulting is susceptible to the same economic cycles as other industries. The main external drivers for the sector are the level of capital investment by the private and public sectors, business and consumer sentiment, and total business profit. In 2020, IBISWorld identified 11 significant consulting practices: McKinsey & Company; Bain & Company; Boston Consulting Group (BCG); Accenture; Roland Berger; Oliver Wyman; LEK; Deloitte; PwC; EY; and KPMG. However, many more noteworthy players are operating globally (Appendix C).

Technological and social development makes clear the need for changes in how we work to drive innovation, adaptability, and resilience and points to the benefits that can accrue due to those changes. In a 2022 survey of 455 firms that "represented all regions of the globe and key executive roles," Deltek and the Hinge Research Institute found that respondents planned to concentrate on efficiency and accuracy. In addition, the stated intentions were to focus on "workflow and process automation, big data, and AI" and to shift away from "cookie-cutter strategies and products" to spend more time on each client and the creation of customised solutions [74, p. 15]. Benefits such as increased execution speed, improved bottom-line results, boosted customer satisfaction, increased productivity, and more engaged employees can all follow. As Sniukas put it, "Companies must prioritize outcomes over procedures, start small, learn, and scale intelligently" [75]. Professional management consultants will continue innovating and driving that change for their clients and themselves.

Those consultancies able to achieve growth above 20% per year are more likely to be medium-sized firms and to be heavier users of marketing and business development technologies to attain high-profit levels [74]. Being able to sustain such growth is a challenge.

Notes

1 This quote is often ascribed to Winston Churchill, but it would seem that he, like others, might have 'borrowed' it from George Russell's "The Irish Homestead."
2 "Permacrisis" is an extended period of uncertainty and insecurity and was selected as Collins Dictionary's "word of the year" for 2022.
3 For more on this topic, review an excellent summary by the editors of History. com, 2020, 'Pandemics That Changed History. As human civilisations rose, these diseases struck them down." https://www.history.com/topics/middle-ages/ pandemics-timeline, accessed 13/09/2020.
4 For more on Taylor and his relevance, see https://hbr.org/1988/11/the-same-old-principles-in-the-new-manufacturing.

Conclusion

So, there you have it. Everything needed for you to start a stellar career as a professional management consultant and thrive in a VUCA world. You should now understand the profession from its beginnings, what a management consultant is and is not, and how and why managers use consultants to effect change and build their businesses. You have also been exposed to what it means to be a professional, the ethical expectations, and your obligations to the role. You have learnt to identify and manage risk and have been introduced to the consulting process from contracting through project execution to closure. Finally, you have been presented with the CMC-Global framework and the professional development pathway required to become certified and an ethical member of an internationally recognised fraternity of advisors to management and governments.

It is a career path that can take you worldwide. My career has taken me to some 50 countries and introduced me to hundreds, perhaps thousands, of interesting people and their challenges. For many, I've been able to help them to plan and implement change that benefitted their businesses. However, not all brought the successes hoped for. From those, my clients and I learnt much, and from failure, we improved. It has been a personally rewarding career.

Your career may take you far and beyond, perhaps even to new worlds. I hope so. Constantly improve your skills and personal awareness, keep to the framework, and maintain your moral compass. Under promise, but over deliver; then success will follow. Good luck!

DOI: 10.4324/9781003466987-11

Appendix A
ICMCI's Members [76]

Member institute	Details
Algeria	www.cmc-global.org/content/algeria
Armenia	www.cmc-global.org/content/institute-management-consulting-armenia
Australia	www.cmc-global.org/content/institute-management-consultants-australia
Austria	www.cmc-global.org/content/austrian-professional-institute-management-consultancy-accounting-and-information-technology
Bangladesh	www.cmc-global.org/content/institute-management-consultants-bangladesh
Brazil	www.cmc-global.org/content/ibco-instituto-brasileiro-dos-consultores-de-organizacao
Bulgaria	www.cmc-global.org/content/bulgarian-association-management-consulting-organizations-bamco
CMC Global Institute	www.cmc-global.org/content/cmc-global-institute-cmc-gi
Canada	www.cmc-global.org/content/cmc-canada
Caribbean	www.cmc-global.org/content/caribbean-institute-certified-management-consultants
China	www.cmc-global.org/content/management-consulting-committee-china-enterprises-confederation
Chinese Taipei	www.cmc-global.org/content/imc-chinese-taipei
Croatia	www.cmc-global.org/node/162
Cyprus	www.cmc-global.org/content/cyprus-institute-certified-management-consultants-cicmc
Finland	www.cmc-global.org/content/finnish-management-consultants-association-liikkeenjohdon-konsultit-ljk-ry
Germany	www.cmc-global.org/node/165
Hong Kong	www.cmc-global.org/content/institute-management-consultants-hong-kong-limited
Hungary	www.cmc-global.org/content/association-management-consultants-hungary-vtmsz
India	www.cmc-global.org/content/institute-management-consultants-india
Iran	www.cmc-global.org/node/183
Ireland	www.cmc-global.org/node/178
Israel	www.cmc-global.org/content/israel-business-consultants-association-ibca

(Continued)

(Continued)

Member institute	Details
Italy	www.cmc-global.org/content/apco-associazione-professionale-italiana-dei-consulenti-di-management
Japan	www.cmc-global.org/content/zen-noh-renall-japan-federation-management-organizations
Jordan	www.cmc-global.org/content/institute-management-consultants-and-trainers-jordan
Kazakhstan	www.cmc-global.org/content/kazakhstan-chamber-management-consultants-cmc-kazakhstan
Korea	www.cmc-global.org/content/kmtcaimc-korea
Kosovo	www.cmc-global.org/content/business-consultants-council-kosovo
Lebanon	www.cmc-global.org/content/imc-lebanon
North Macedonia	www.cmc-global.org/content/management-consulting-association-2000
Mongolia	www.cmc-global.org/content/imc-mongolia
Netherlands	www.cmc-global.org/content/orde-van-organisatiekundigen-en-adviseurs-ooa
New Zealand	www.cmc-global.org/content/institute-management-consultants-new-zealand-inc
Nigeria	www.cmc-global.org/content/institute-management-consultants-nigeria
Philippines	www.cmc-global.org/content/institute-certified-management-consultants-philippines
Romania	www.cmc-global.org/node/168
Russia	www.cmc-global.org/content/national-institute-certified-management-consultants-nicmc
Serbia	www.cmc-global.org/content/association-management-consultants-serbia-upks
Singapore	www.cmc-global.org/content/institute-management-consultants-singapore
South Africa	www.cmc-global.org/node/180
Sweden	www.cmc-global.org/content/swedish-association-management-consultants
Switzerland	www.cmc-global.org/content/asco-ass-management-consultants-switzerland
Thailand	www.cmc-global.org/node/193
Turkey	www.cmc-global.org/node/196
Ukraine	www.cmc-global.org/content/institute-management-consultants-ukraine
United Kingdom	www.cmc-global.org/content/institute-consulting-uk
United States	www.cmc-global.org/node/177
Zimbabwe	www.cmc-global.org/node/177

Appendix B
CMC-Global Succession History

Country	Time served		Name	Role1	Role2	Role3	Role4
USA	1987	1991	Roethle, John D	Chair/ Immediate Past Chair			
UK	1987	1993	Thomas, Hedley	Vice Chair	Chair/ Immediate Past Chair		
Canada	1987	1995	Amar, David	Vice Chair	Chair/ Immediate Past Chair		
Austria	1989	1991	Leissenger, Otto	Treasurer			
Australia	1989	1991	Smith, Geoffrey	Secretary			
USA	1989	1997	Shays, Michael	Vice Chair	Chair/ Immediate Past Chair		
Canada	1991	1997	Brouillard, Bob	Treasurer	Vice Chair	Secretary	
UK	1991	1999	Tindley, Denis	Vice Chair	Chair/ Immediate Past Chair		
India	1991	2001	Viera, Walter	Vice Chair	Secretary	Chair/ Immediate Past Chair	
Netherlands	1991	2003	de Sonnaville, Hans	Secretary	Vice Chair	Treasurer	Chair/ Immediate Past Chair
USA	1993	1997	Cali, Vincent	Treasurer	Vice Chair		
Australia	1995	2005	Elliot, Richard	Vice Chair	Chair/ Immediate Past Chair		
Canada	1997	1999	Czamanske, Paul	Treasurer			
Canada	1997	2003	Haight, Lynn	Vice Chair	Treasurer		
South Africa & UK	1997	2007	Curnow, Barry	Secretary			
South Africa	1999	2003	Kehayas, Angelo	Secretary	Vice Chair		
Denmark	1999	2009	Sorensen, Peter	Vice Chair	Treasurer	Chair/ Immediate Past Chair	

(*Continued*)

(Continued)

Country	Time served		Name	Role1	Role2	Role3	Role4
India	2001	2003	Gopalkrishnan, Shanker	Vice Chair			
Austria	2001	2007	Prechtl, Gerd	Vice Chair			
Singapore	2003	2005	Goh, Kim Seng	Secretary			
Italy	2003	2005	Guazzoni, Franco	Vice Chair			
Singapore	2003	2005	Ng, Garry	Treasurer			
Netherlands	2003	2007	Roels, Alphons	Vice Chair	Treasurer		
India	2005	2006	Gopalkrishnan, Shanker	Vice Chair			
UK	2005	2011	Ing, Brian	Secretary	Chair/ Immediate Past Chair		
Singapore	2005	2011	Liew, Shin Liat	Vice Chair			
Austria	2006	2013	Ennsfellner, Ilse	Vice Chair			
Italy	2006	2015	D'Aprile, Francesco	Vice Chair	Chair/ Immediate Past Chair		
Canada	2007	2011	Nesbitt, Mark	Secretary			
India	2007	2013	Madhok, Aneeta	Vice Chair	Chair/ Immediate Past Chair		
UK	2007	2013	Markham, Calvert	Vice Chair			
Netherlands	2007	2013	Wagenaar, Rob	Treasurer	Vice Chair		
Australia	2009	2018	Millar, Tim	Vice Chair	Chair/ Immediate Past Chair		
Croatia	2011	2013	Barisic, Anton	Vice Chair			
Canada	2011	2013	Harris, Richard	Vice Chair			
Taiwan	2011	2013	Liu, Charles	Vice Chair			
USA	2011	2013	McNaughton, Drumm	Secretary			
Romania	2011	2021	Caian, Sorin	Treasurer	Vice Chair	Chair/ Immediate Past Chair	
Thailand	2013	2015	Hytanuwatra, Chayaditt	Vice Chair			
UK	2013	2015	Ing, Brian	Secretary			
Finland	2013	2019	Karme, Kim	Vice Chair	Secretary		
Ukraine	2013	2019	Yuzkova, Elena	Vice Chair	Director		
Austria	**2013**	**Current**	**Bodenstein, Rob**	**Vice Chair**	**Director**	**Chair/ Immediate Past Chair**	
Canada	**2013**	**Current**	**Mihalicz, Dwight**	**Treasurer**	**Chair/ Immediate Past Chair**		
USA	2015	2017	Matar, Oliver	Chair/ Immediate Past Chair			

(*Continued*)

(Continued)

Country	Time served		Name	Role1	Role2	Role3	Role4
Republic of Korea	2015	2021	Han, Kyeonh Seok	Vice Chair	Director		
UK	2015	2022	Webster, Jeremy	Vice Chair	Director	Secretary	
Netherlands	2017	2021	Kradolfer, Jan Willem	Vice Chair	Director	Treasurer	
Romania	2018	2019	Bors, Anca	Treasurer			
China	2019	2022	Yanyan, Zhang	Director			
Kosovo	2019	2023	Lluka, Jehona	Director			
Bulgaria	**2019**	**Current**	**Mantarkova, Gergana**	**Director**			
Jordan	**2021**	**Current**	**Abdel-Jaber, Tamara**	**Treasurer**			
Australia	**2021**	**Current**	**Blackman, Alan**	**Director**			
UK	**2021**	**Current**	**Warn, Nick**	**Director**	**Secretary**		
Switzerland	**2022**	**Current**	**Huesler, Ruggero**	**Director**			
Caribbean	**2022**	**Current**	**Shorey, Norma**	**Director**			
Serbia	**2023**	**Current**	**Hristov, Aleksandra**	**Director**			

Appendix C
Top 35 Consulting Practices in 2021

A composite alphabetical list of the top 35 in 2021 is shown below [77–78]:

Organisation	Consultancy Type
Accenture https://www.accenture.com/au-en/about/company-index	Tier 2: Accounting, finance, and technology
AlixPartners https://www.alixpartners.com/about-alixpartners/	Operations and turnaround
Alvarez & Marsal https://www.alvarezandmarsal.com/	Operations and turnaround
Analysis Group https://www.analysisgroup.com/careers/join-us/	Economic and litigation consulting.
Bain https://www.bain.com/	Tier 1: Strategy, plus many other
Barkawi Management Consultants https://www.barkawi.com/en/start.html	Function/industry focussed.
Booz Allen Hamilton https://www.boozallen.com/	Accounting, finance, and technology
Bridgespan Group https://www.bridgespan.org/	Function/industry focussed, non-profit sector consulting
Capgemini SE https://www.capgemini.com/se-en/	Function/industry focussed technology
ClearView Healthcare Partners https://clearviewhcp.com/	Function/industry focussed, healthcare/med-tech
Deloitte https://www2.deloitte.com/global/en/services/consulting-deloitte.html	Big 4: Accounting, finance, and technology
Ernst & Young (EY) https://managementconsulted.com/consulting-firm/ernst-young/	Big 4: General management and strategy, accounting, finance, and technology

(*Continued*)

(Continued)

Organisation	Consultancy Type
Ernst & Young LLP (EY-Parthenon) https://www.ey.com/en_gl/strategy/ about-ey-parthenon	General management and strategy
Gartner Inc https://www.gartner.com/en/consulting	Tier 2: General management, marketing, research, and technology
Guidehouse https://guidehouse.com/	Function/industry focussed
IBM Global Business Service https://www.ibm.com/services/business	Tier 2: Strategy, operations, and technology
Implement Consulting Group P/s https://implementconsultinggroup.com/	Strategy and transformation, operational efficiency, digitalisation and IT, leadership and change, growth and innovation
Insight Sourcing Group https://managementconsulted.com/ insight-sourcing-group/	Function/industry focussed strategic sourcing and procurement.
Kearney https://www.kearney.com/	Tier 2: Global strategic partnerships, social impact and sustainability, function/ industry focussed
KPMG International https://home.kpmg/xx/en/home.html	Big 4: Accounting, finance, and technology
LEK Consulting https://www.lek.com/	Tier 2: General management and strategy
McKinsey & Company, Inc. https://www.mckinsey.com/	Tier 1: Strategy and many other
Mercer https://www.mercer.com/	HR and finance
Oliver Wyman https://www.oliverwyman.com/index.html	Tier 2: General management and strategy
Pöyry PLC https://www.environmental-expert.com/ companies/poeyry-plc-5769	Function/industry focussed, international consulting, and engineering
Putnam Consulting https://putnam-consulting.com/	Function/industry focussed; philanthropy
PwC Consulting https://www.pwc.com/id/en/services/consulting. html	Accounting, finance, and technology
Ramboll Group A/S https://ramboll.com/	Engineering and design consulting

(*Continued*)

(Continued)

Organisation	Consultancy Type
Roland Berger https://www.rolandberger.com/en/?country=GB	Tier 2: General management and strategy
Solon Management Consulting https://solonmanagement.com	Boutique media and telecoms consulting.
Strategy & (formerly Booz & Company, now part of PwC) https://www.strategyand.pwc.com/	General management & strategy
Tata Consultancy Services https://www.tcs.com/	Finance, operations, communications, and technology
The Boston Consulting Group Inc. (BCG) https://www.bcg.com/	Tier 1: Strategy, plus many other
Wavestone https://www.wavestone.com/en/	Accounting, finance, and technology
Wikistrat https://www.wikistrat.com/	Boutique crowd-sourced consulting

Appendix D
Code of Professional Conduct and Ethics

Preamble

The Institute of Management Consultants Ltd (IMC) in Australia adopted the following Code of Ethics on 12th November 2016 as proof of the commitment of IMC Members to:

- Develop realistic and practical solutions to client problems.
- Act in the client's best interests at all times.
- Render impartial, factually based, independent advice.
- Accept only those client engagements they are qualified to perform.
- Behave with integrity and professionalism at all times.
- Agree with the client in advance based on their professional fees.
- Safeguard confidential information.

As the professional association and certifying body for management consultants in Australia, the Institute of Management Consultants (IMC) requires adherence to this Code of Ethics as a condition of membership and a prerequisite to certification. All members have pledged in writing to abide by the Institute's Code of Ethics, and their voluntary adherence to the Code signifies the self-discipline of the profession (Appendix D).

The Code sets out the principles of the ethical practice of management consulting. This Code ensures IMC members maintain professionalism and adhere to high ethical standards while providing services to clients and dealings with their colleagues and the public.

The individual judgement of member consultants is required to apply these principles, and members may be liable for disciplinary action under the IMC rules if their conduct is found to:

- violate the Code or
- bring discredit to the profession or the IMC.

The Disciplinary Committee of the Institute will investigate any such complaint and, amongst other options, may sanction or expel the member if a breach is confirmed.

Code of Ethics

1   Each member's objective as a professional management consultant is to assist their clients by adding value to the client's enterprise, whether it takes the form of a business, a not-for-profit organisation, or an element of government.

2   A member will serve their clients with integrity, competence, objectivity, independence, and professionalism.

3   A member will only accept assignments that the member is competent to perform. They will only assign staff or engage colleagues with knowledge and expertise relevant to the client project.

4   Before accepting any engagement, a member will establish the realistic client expectations of the assignment's objectives, scope, expected benefits, work plan, and fee structure.

5   A member will agree with the client on fees and expenses in advance. A member will charge reasonable fees commensurate with the services delivered, the value created, and the risk or responsibility accepted.

6   A member recognises that the client's enterprise has many stakeholders whose interests are sometimes divergent. Therefore, they will seek to balance and reconcile these different interests in their guidance to the client.

7   A member's advice to the client will be delivered with independence and courage, always focussing on the long-term best interests of the client enterprise, even when this guidance may lead to actions such as restructuring or reductions that may be painful in the short term.

8   A member will continually invest in professional development to keep abreast of evolving knowledge within their profession and in areas of technical expertise.

9   A member will treat all confidential client information appropriately, take reasonable steps to prevent access to personal information by unauthorised people, and not take advantage of proprietary or privileged information for use by the member or others without the client's permission.

10 A member will avoid conflicts of interest or the appearance of such and immediately disclose to the client any circumstances or claims they believe may influence their judgment or objectivity.

11 A member will offer to withdraw from a consulting assignment when they believe their objectivity or integrity may be impaired.

12 A member will represent the profession with integrity and professionalism in their relations with clients, colleagues, and the general public.

13 A member will respect the rights of consulting colleagues and firms and will not use their proprietary information or methodologies without permission.

14 A member will not accept commissions, remuneration, or other benefits from a third party in connection with any recommendations to a client without that client's prior knowledge and consent and will disclose in advance any financial interests in goods or services that form part of such recommendations.

15 A member will refrain from inviting an active or inactive client employee to consider alternative employment without prior discussion with the client.

16 Members will not deceptively advertise their services or misrepresent or denigrate individual consulting practitioners, consulting firms, or professionals.

17 A member will promote adherence to the Code of Ethics by all consultants working on their behalf.

A client, a member of the public, or a member of the Institute may report a perceived violation of the Code of Ethics to the Institute of Management Consultants. If such a complaint is received, the institute will convene a disciplinary committee to investigate and recommend appropriate actions. Such actions may include but are not limited to mediation, arbitration, or sanction against the member concerned.

Appendix E
The Consultant's Pledge

As a management consultant, my professional objective is to assist my clients in adding value to their enterprise, whether that enterprise takes the form of a business, a not-for-profit organisation, or an element of government.

I pledge to uphold and promote the IMC Code of Ethics in all my consulting activities.

I will serve my clients with integrity, competence, objectivity, independence, and professionalism.

I will only accept assignments that I am competent to perform. I will only assign staff or engage colleagues with knowledge and expertise appropriate to that client's needs on a project.

I will establish realistic expectations of the benefits and results of my services with my clients. Together, we will define the scope and process of the assignment and the basis of remuneration. I pledge that considerations of personal benefit will never override my focus on the client's interests or stakeholders.

I promise to uphold both the letter and the spirit of laws, regulations, and contracts governing my conduct, that of my client, and the societies in which we operate. My behaviour will exemplify the values I publicly espouse in making this pledge.

I will be equally vigilant in ensuring the professional behaviour of other consultants within my practice or the wider IMC membership. I will bring to attention any violation of this shared professional code.

I will not permit considerations of race, gender, nationality, religion, politics, sexual orientation, or social status to influence my professional behaviour or advice. I will respect those whose well-being may depend on my decisions or direction. I will diligently apply objective judgment to all consulting assignments based on the best information. I will conduct independent research and analysis and consult with colleagues and others to help inform my decision.

I will continually invest in professional development to keep abreast of evolving knowledge within my profession and my areas of technical expertise.

I recognise that my status and privileges as a professional stem from the respect and trust that the profession enjoys. Accordingly, I accept my responsibility to employ, protect, and develop the above standards to enhance that respect and trust.

I do so solemnly pledge.

Appendix F
Key Financial Statement Analysis Ratios

Ratio	Ratio formula
Liquidity	
Current ratio	*Current assets*
	Current liabilities
Quick (acid-test) ratio	*Cash+liquid assets+receivables*
	Current liabilities
Net working capital	Current assets – current liabilities
Profitability	
Gross profit margin	*Gross profit*
	Sales
Net profit margin	*Net profit (income)*
	Net sales
Return on total assets	*Net income*
	Average total sales
Return on equity (ROE)	*Net income*
	Shareholder's equity
EBITDA	Net income + interest expenses + tax + depreciation + amortisation
EBITDA margin	*EBITDA*
	Sales×100
Activity	
Accounts receivable turnover	*Net credit sales*
	Average accounts receivable
Average collection period	*365*
	Accounts receivable turnover
Inventory turnover	*Cost of goods sold*
	Average inventory
Average age of inventory	*365*
	Inventory turnover
Total asset turnover	*Net sales*
	Average total assets

(*Continued*)

(Continued)

Ratio	Ratio formula
Leverage	
Debt ratio	*Total liabilities*
	Total assets
Debt to equity ratio	*Total liabilities*
	Shareholders' equity
Interest coverage ratio (times interest earned)	*Earnings before interest and taxes*
	Interest expense
Equity ratio	*Total equity*
	Total assets

Appendix G
Some Applicable Guidelines and International Standards[1]

Guidelines

- Customer satisfaction – ISO 10008
- Organisational culture – ISO 10010
- Guidelines for consultants and use of their services – ISO 10019
- Organisational change management – ISO 10020
- Guidelines for management consulting services – ISO 20700
- Risk management – ISO 31000
- Governance – ISO 37000

ISO MS Standards

- ISO 9001 – Quality management
- ISO 14001 and related standards – Environmental management
- ISO 19011 – Auditing management systems – first, second, and third party
- ISO 22301 – Business continuity and resilience
- IS0 27001 – Information security – required for Defence Industry Security Program accreditation to supply
- ISO 28001 – Supply chain security
- ISO 44001 – Collaborative business relationships
- ISO 50001 – Energy management
- ISO 55001 – Asset management

Handbooks

- ISO integrated use of management system standards:https://www.iso.org/news/ref2347.html Preview https://www.iso.org/publication/PUB100435.html
- Standards Australia – SA HB 186 The Stakeholder Approach to Organizational Sustainability https://www.techstreet.com/standards/sa-hb-186-2019?product_id=2076903

Note

1 Available from www.iso.org/standard

Glossary

5-Forces analysis
Academic Fellow
Academic Fellows Faculty
Accenture
Alan Blackman
Ambiguity
Arthur Andersen
Bain
black swan
Bond University
Booz Allen & Hamilton
Boston Consulting Group
Boyd's 1974 OODA loop
Business structures
Carl Jung
Certified Management Consultant (CMC)
CMC
Code of Conduct
Code of Ethics
Colonel Urwick
Competence
competency
Competency Framework
Critical and creative thinking
Deloitte
Ethics
Expression of Interest (EOI).
EY
Five Forces Model
Frank Gilbert
Gantt chart
Griffith Business School
Harvard Business School
Harvard University
Hiatt's ADKAR model
IBISWorld
IBM

(*Continued*)

(Continued)

Institute of Management Consultants
ISO 26000:2010
ISO 27001
ISO20700:2017
James McKinsey
John Searcy-Hammond
Keirsey Temperament Sorter
KPMG
Leading and managing change
LEK
Lillian Gilbreth
Marvin Bower
Massachusetts Institute of Technology (MIT)
McKinsey & Co.
McKinsey & Company
Myers-Briggs Type Indicator®
National Consulting Index
Oliver Wyman
P.A. Consulting
P.A. Management Consultants
PE Consulting Group Australia
Personnel Administration (P.A.)
PEST
PESTEL analysis
Peter Westlund
Porter's 5-Forces Analysis
Price Waterhouse
Price Waterhouse, Coopers, Lybrand
pricing model
PwC
Request for a quotation (RFQ)
risk assessment
Roland Berger
Scientific Management movement
Source Global Research
Stephen Hawking
SWOT
SWOT analysis
Terms of Reference
Trust
United Nations Economic and Social Council
value proposition
W.D. Scott
W.D. Scott & Co.

Bibliography

1 Beaton, G., *Why professionalism matters more than ever*. 2022, Melbourne, VIC: Australian Council of Professions.

2 Schwenker, K., et al., in *Management consulting. An introduction to the methodologies, tools and techniques of the profession*, J. Hunter, et al., Editors. 2009, Toronto, Canada: CMC - Canada.

3 Barry, M., Management consulting in Australia, in *Australian Industry (ANZSIC) Report*. 2022, IBISWorld.

4 Haslam, S., Developing the national consulting index: An update on how to estimate the size of national management consulting sectors. *Management Consulting Journal*, 2022. **3**(1): pp. 105–110.

5 Haslam, S., et al., Developing a national consulting index (NCI), in *International Consultants' Day 2022*. 2022, Vienna, Austria: ICMCI.

6 Haslam, S., R. Bodenstein, and T. Abdel-Jaber, *ICMCI national consultancy index - estimating the size of management consulting markets around the world*. 2022, International Council of Management Consulting Institutes.

7 Haslam, S. and A. Blackman. ICMCI National consulting index global report, in *International Consultants Day*. 2023, Online (Zoom): ICMCI.

8 ICMCI. *Global management consulting community*. 2022 [cited 2022 22 June]; Organisation website. Available from: https://www.cmc-global.org/content/global-management-consulting-community.

9 Gimmig, M., et al., *Management consulting. An introduction to the methodologies, tools and techniques of the profession*. Australian and New Zealand ed, J. Bielenberg, et al., Editors. 2020, Surrey Hills, VIC: IMC Australia.

10 IMC_Australia, *Memorandum of association of institute of management consultants ACN 000 628 884*. 1969, Sydney, NSW: Institute_of_Management_Consultants.

11 IMC_Australia, *Constitution of institute of management consultants*. 2020, Brisbane, QLD: Institute_of_Management_Consultants.

12 Turner, S., *IMC – ACoP*. 2022, Brisbane, QLD: Alan Blackman.

13 Beeby, J. and Z. Stumpf, *The Australian consulting market in 2022*. 2022, London, UK: Source Global Research.

14 ICMCI, *International congress of management consulting institutes minutes*. 1987, Paris, France: ICMCI.

15 CMC-Global, *Succession history* [Website] 2023 [cited 2023 9 July]; Organisation web page. Available from: https://www.cmc-global.org/content/succession-history.

16 Nasser, R., *ICMCI history question*, A.J. Blackman, Editor. 2022, Amman, Jordan: ICMCI.

17 ICMCI, *The ICMCI - 25 years of achievement 1987-2012*, A. Kehayas, Editor. 2012, Zurich, Switzerland: ICMCI.

18 CMC-Global, *List of previous CMC-global events locations*. [Website] 2023 [cited 2023 9 July]; Organisation web page. Available from: https://www.cmc-global.org/content/list-previous-cmc-global-events-locations.

19 Westlund, P.N., *IMC answers to questions on notice to the inquiry into the management and assurance of integrity by consulting services*. 2023, Melbourne, VIC: Institute of Management Consultants (Australia).

20 Warn, N. and C. Seçkin, The new CMC manual 2022: "Excellence in Consultancy", in *New CMC standards – update webinars*. 2022, ICMCI Professional Standards Committee: Online.

21 Mihalicz, D.W., *ICMCI governance review task force report*. 2022, Zurich, Switzerland: International Council of Management Consulting Institutes.

22 Haslam, S., *Re Australian Senate enquiry*, A. Blackman, Editor. 2023, Gmail.

23 Mishkin, B., *Everything they had: Sports writing*, in *One on 1*. D. Halberstam, Editor. 2007, New York, NY: Hyperion.

24 Smith, R.C., *Mind for hire. A practitioner's guide to management consulting*. 2000, Nedlands, WA: University of Western Australia Press.

25 Smith, K., An expert – Common key characteristics. *Academia Letters*, 2021 (Article 4181).

26 Dawson, R., *Developing knowledge-based client relationships: Leadership in professional services*. 2nd ed. 2005, Oxford, UK: Elsevier Butterworth-Heinemann.

27 ILO, *Management consulting – A guide to the profession*. 4th ed, M. Kubr, Editor. 2002, New Delhi: Bookwell Publications.

28 Rittel, H.W.J. and M.M. Webber, Dilemmas in a general theory of planning. *Policy Sciences*, 1973. **4**(2): pp. 155–169.

29 Camillus, J.C., *Strategy as a wicked problem*. Harvard Business Review, 2008.

30 Cerruti, C., E. Tavoletti, and C. Grieco, Management consulting: a review of fifty years of scholarly research. *Management Research Review*, 2019. **42**(8): pp. 902–925.

31 Furusten, S., Management consultants as improvising agents of stability. *Scandinavian Journal of Management*, 2009. **25**(3): pp. 265–285.

32 Westlund, P., *Review of professional management consulting publication*, A.J. Blackman, Editor. 2022, Brisbane, QLD: Dr Alan Blackman.

33 Šola, T., *Eternity does not live here any more – A glossary of museum sins*. 2012, Zagreb: Self-released.

34 *Merriam-Webster Dictionary*, 2022 [cited 2022 7 March]; Available from: https://www.merriam-webster.com/dictionary/professional.

35 *Oxford Learners Dictionary*. 2022; Available from: https://www.oxfordlearnersdictionaries.com/definition/american_english/professional_2#:~:text=Definition%20of%20professional%20noun%20from%20the%20Oxford%20Advanced,need%20a%20professional%20to%20sort%20out%20your%20finances.

36 Maister, D., R. Galford, and C. Green, *The trusted advisor*. 20th Anniversary ed. 2021, Boston, MA: Free Press/Simon & Schuster. 336.

37 White, R.W., Motivation reconsidered: The concept of competence. *Psychological Review*, 1959. **66**(5): pp. 297–333.

38 United_Nations, *Sustainable development goals*. 2022 [cited 2022 9 September]; Available from: https://sdgs.un.org/goals#goals.

39 ISO, *Guidance on social responsibility*. 2020 [cited 2022 9 September]; Available from: https://www.iso.org/iso-26000-social-responsibility.html.

40 ISO, *ISO 20700:2017(E): Guidelines for management consultancy services*. 2017, Geneva, Switzerland: ISO. V.

41 ICMCI, *Code of conduct*. 2021 21 January [cited 2022 06 July]; Available from: https://www.cmc-global.org/content/icmci-code-conduct.

42 IMC_Australia, *Our mission*. IMC Strategic Plan 2018–2021 2018 [cited 2022 6 March]; Available from: https://www.imc.org.au/Web/About/Mission-Strategy/Web/Mission-Strategy.aspx?hkey=fca486b2-de1c-47ad-bc10-c282c87ff680.

43 Unknown. *The myers & briggs foundation*. 2022 [cited 2022 22 July]; Organisation website. Available from: https://www.myersbriggs.org/.

44 Keirsey, D. and M. Bates, *Please understand me: Character and temperament types*. 1984, Prometheus Nemesis Book Company.

45 Birkman. *The Birkman method: Four perspectives of personality*. 2022 [cited 2022 9 September]; Available from: https://birkman.com/the-birkman-method/.

46 Porter, M.E., *Competitive strategy: Techniques for analyzing industries and competitors*. 1980, New York: Free Press.

47 Pfeffer, J., *The human equation: Building Profits by putting people first*. 1998, Harvard Business Press.

48 Taleb, N.N., *The black swan: The impact of the highly improbable*. 2nd ed. 2010, New York: Random House Trade Paperbacks.

49 Cattell, J., et al., *A theory of everything: Rebuilding the consulting model, capability by capability*. 2020, London, UK: S.I.S. Ltd.

50 ACARA. *Critical and creative thinking*. 2022 [cited 2022 20 March]; Version 8.4. Available from: https://www.australiancurriculum.edu.au/f-10-curriculum/general-capabilities/critical-and-creative-thinking/.

51 USAID, *Change Management best practices guide: An additional help for ADS Chapter 597*, U.S.A.f.I.D. (USAID), Editor. 2015, USAID: Online.

52 Burnes, B., M. Hughes, and R.T. By, Reimagining organisational change leadership. *Leadership*, 2016(0): pp. 1–18.

53 Kotter, J.P., Leading change. Why transformation efforts fail, in *Museum management and marketing*, R. Sandell and R.R. Janes, Editors. 2007, Routledge.com.

54 Kotter, J.P., *8 Steps to accelerate change in your organisation*. 2022, Seatle, WA: Kotter Inc (Online).

55 Hiatt, J.M. and T.J. Creasey, *Change management: The people side of change*. 2012, Loveland, CO: Prosci Inc.

56 CMC-Global, *Certified management consultant (CMC) competency framework overview*. 2021, Geneva, Switzerland: The International Council of Management Consulting Institutes. p. 2.

57 Voss, C. and T. Raz, *Never split the difference: Negotiating as if your life depended on it*. 2016, London, UK: Random House.

58 Dennis, F., *How to get rich: One of the World's greatest entrepreneurs shares his secrets*. Kindle ed. 2006: Penguin Publishing Group.

59 Jamison, K.R., *An unquiet mind: A memoir of moods and madness*. Picador Classic. 2015, New York: Picador.

60 Australia. *Application-AU Business Number*. [Webpage] 2020 [cited 2023 29 May]; Web page. Available from: https://smepro-australia.com/?msclkid=c200928e2f6f1c7c460cf6fdf669b076.

61 Maister, D., *Practice what you preach: What managers must do to create a high achievement culture*. 2001, New York: The Free Press.

62 Lanning, M.J. and E.G. Michaels, A business is a value delivery system. *McKinsey Staff Paper*, 1988. **41**: pp. 53–57.

63 Twin, A. *Value proposition: How to write it with examples*. Business Essentials [Corporate website] 2023 17 March [cited 2023 5 May]; Available from: https://www.investopedia.com/terms/v/valueproposition.asp.

64 Mazzacato, M., Public submission to the finance and public administration references committee inquiry into the management and assurance of integrity by consulting services, in *Senate inquiry into the management and assurance of integrity by consulting services*. 2023, Canberra, ACT: Australian Government. pp. 1–6.

65 McIlroy, T., Big four consulting firms face new inquiry over PwC tax leaks, in *Australian Financial Review*. 2023, Melbourne, VIC: Fairfax Press.

66 Tadros, E., Professor James Guthrie wants a central Commonwealth body to manage consultant use, in *Australian Financial Review*. 2023, Melbourne, VIC: Fairfax Press.

67 Bourgeois, T., *The global consulting marketplace. Key data, forecasts & trends 2004-2006*. Kennedy Information ed. 2004, Peterborough, NH: IBM Consulting Services.

68 Russell, G.W., *The Irish homestead: The organ of Irish agricultural and industrial development*. Notes of the Week: Fair Play in Legislation, G.W. Russell, Editor. Vol. 17, Number 53. 1910, Dublin, Ireland: Irish Agricultural Organisation Society.

69 McKinsey&Company, *Governments face a $30 trillion fiscal gap by 2023*. Charting the path to the next normal 2020 30 July [cited 2022 18 February]; Available from: https://www.mckinsey.com/featured-insights/coronavirus-leading-through-the-crisis/charting-the-path-to-the-next-normal/governments-face-a-30-trillion-fiscal-gap-by-2023.

70 Yue, L. *PRESS RELEASE—At doom's doorstep: It is 100 seconds to midnight*. 2022 [cited 2022 20 January]; Available from: https://thebulletin.org/2022/01/press-release-at-dooms-doorstep-it-is-100-seconds-to-midnight/.

71 Ghosh, P. *Hawking says Trump's climate stance could damage Earth*. 2017 2 July [cited 2022 2 March]; Available from: https://www.bbc.com/news/science-environment-40461726.

72 Kharpal, A. *Here are 4 of Stephen Hawking's biggest predictions from human extinction to aliens*. Yahoo!Finance 2018 15 March [cited 2022 18 February]; Available from: https://finance.yahoo.com/news/4-stephen-hawking-apos-biggest-131400979.html.

73 Deltek, *High growth study 2022. Consulting services edition*. 2022. Hinge Research Institute.

74 Sniukas, M., *The human-centric organization: What it is and why you should you care*. 2022, Amman, Jordan: CMC-Global. https://youtu.be/mMYxVqVEf_w.

75 ICMCI, *Member Institutes*. 2022 [cited 2022 21 September]; Available from: https://www.cmc-global.org/content/member-institutes.

76 IBISWorld, Management consulting in Australia – Market research report, in *Industry research reports – Australia*. 2021, Sydney, NSW: IBISWorld.

77 Tran, K., *Top consulting firms [2020 Ranking] by overall vault ranking, salary, prestige, work/life balance, industry expertise, revenue, and more*. 2020 [cited 2022 18 February]; Available from: https://mconsultingprep.com/top-management-consulting-ranking/.

78 *Top 25 Consulting Firms*. 2022 [cited 2022 20 February]; Available from: https://managementconsulted.com/top-25-consulting-firms/#:~:text=1%20Kearney.%20Kearney%20%28formerly%20known%20as%20A.T.%20...,Company%2C%20which%20was%20acquired%20by%20PwC%20in%202014.

Index

For Product Safety Concerns and Information please contact our
EU representative GPSR@taylorandfrancis.com Taylor & Francis
Verlag GmbH, Kaufingerstraße 24, 80331 München, Germany